Julius Caesar

The World Generals Series

"Palgrave's World Generals Series features great leaders whose reputations have transcended their own nations, whose bold characters led to new forms of combat, whose determination and courage gave shape to new dynasties and civilizations—men whose creativity and courage inspired multitudes. Beginning with illustrious World War II German Field Marshal Erwin Rommel, known as the Desert Fox, the series sheds new light on famous warrior-leaders such as Alexander, Julius Caesar, and Lafayette, drawing out the many important leadership lessons that are still relevant to our lives today."

—*General Wesley K. Clark (Ret.)*

This distinguished new series features the lives of eminent military leaders from around the world who changed history. Top military historians are writing concise but comprehensive biographies including the personal lives, battles, strategies, and legacies of these great generals, with the aim to provide background and insight into contemporary armies and wars, as well as to draw lessons for the leaders of today.

Rommel by Charles Messenger

Alexander the Great by Bill Yenne

Montgomery by Trevor Royle

Lafayette by Marc Leepson

Ataturk by Austin Bay

De Gaulle by Michael E. Haskew

Julius Caesar by Bill Yenne

Julius Caesar

Lessons in Leadership from the Great Conqueror

Bill Yenne

palgrave
macmillan

JULIUS CAESAR
Copyright © Bill Yenne, 2012.

First published in 2012 by
PALGRAVE MACMILLAN®
in the U.S.—a division of St. Martin's Press LLC,
175 Fifth Avenue, New York, NY 10010.

Where this book is distributed in the UK, Europe and the rest of the world,
this is by Palgrave Macmillan, a division of Macmillan Publishers Limited,
registered in England, company number 785998, of Houndmills,
Basingstoke, Hampshire RG21 6XS.

Palgrave Macmillan is the global academic imprint of the above companies
and has companies and representatives throughout the world.

Palgrave® and Macmillan® are registered trademarks in the United States,
the United Kingdom, Europe and other countries.

ISBN: 978–0–230–11231–5

Library of Congress Cataloging-in-Publication Data

Yenne, Bill, 1949–
    Julius Caesar : lessons in leadership from the great conqueror /
Bill Yenne; foreword by Wesley K. Clark.
        p. cm.—(The world generals series)
    Includes bibliographical references and index.
    ISBN 978–0–230–11231–5 (hardback)
        1. Caesar, Julius. 2. Caesar, Julius—Military leadership. 3. Caesar,
Julius—Influence. 4. Political leadership—Rome—Case studies. 5. Heads
of state—Rome—Biography. 6. Generals—Rome—Biography. 7. Rome—
Kings and rulers—Biography. 8. Rome—History—Republic, 265–30 B.C.
9. Rome—Politics and government—265–30 B.C. 10. Rome—History,
Military—265–30 B.C. I. Title.

DG262.Y46 2012
937'.05092—dc23
[B]   2011031584

A catalogue record of the book is available from the British Library.

Design by Newgen Imaging Systems (P) Ltd., Chennai, India

First edition: January 2012

10 9 8 7 6 5 4 3 2 1

Printed in the United States of America.

Contents

*Eight pages of black-and-white illustrations appear
between pages 118 and 119.*

Foreword

Julius Caesar: probably one of the two greatest soldier-statesman in history. Through his conquests he brought civilization to Western Europe and laid the basis for modern Western civilization while maintaining the unity and grandeur of Rome. As a young man, he looked up to Alexander the Great but far surpassed him in the breadth of his achievements, and he was admired and emulated, mostly unsuccessfully, for the next twenty centuries.

While most have heard of Caesar, Bill Yenne's crisp, sparkling biography lays out the campaigns, the intrigues, and the outcomes amid the blizzard of unpronounceable names and antique geography as well as it has ever been done. And through the record of his achievements, much of which is captured through Caesar's own writings, his extraordinary character and abilities show through.

As a warrior, Caesar was extraordinarily competent and battle-proven at "every level of command," as we like to say today. As an individual warrior he was sufficiently skilled and fierce to lead from the front and plunge directly into the battle himself if necessary—he won the equivalent of today's Congressional Medal of Honor as a young officer by saving a fellow legionnaire. But he fought at the front rank not only as a young man but even as an aging middle-aged commander, who, in his mid-fifties, plunged into the clash of sword and shield in personal combat. How he maintained his skill and conditioning for close combat is one of the marvels of his career that few who followed have ever matched.

He also had extraordinary endurance and stamina, campaigning without let-up for years, traveling on horseback, boat, and foot from Britain, Switzerland, Croatia, Italy, and back, when every wearying mile exerted its toll and imposed its hardships and risks. He did it year after year. By our standards today, Caesar and his subordinates would probably rank as athletes of Olympic caliber, playing professional sports into their fifties.

But it was his tactical acumen, strategic brilliance, and insights that made him unique. From his earliest episodes of combat as a young man on the run from an aging emperor to the seasoned warrior, he saw the battlefield in unusual depth. He wasn't particularly "formulaic," or doctrinaire, despite having Rome's outstanding military organizations behind him. Instead he brought his judgment to bear on each challenge as a unique situation and used the standard operating procedures and skills of his legions with imagination and agility. In one case he might seize the initiative; in another he might go on the defensive. He could command a few cohorts effectively in a foraging skirmish, while maintaining simultaneously his command grip on legions dispersed throughout Gaul, as well as the politics of Rome. He was a master at the use of quick combat engineering, in the form of earthworks, bridges, and boats. He excelled in opportunism, but was as vigorous and insightful in the strategic defense as in the head-rush of the attack. He pursued adversaries relentlessly but minded his logistics and avoided becoming over-extended.

Modern generals of the twentieth and twenty-first centuries might command for a campaign or two, but Caesar was at the highest rank for some fifteen years. There's simply no one else since who's done so much, and so successfully. Not MacArthur, Patton, or Eisenhower. Not Napoleon, or Rommel. Not the pretenders like Adolf Hitler. Not Stalin, Mao, or Zhukov. In his martial success, Caesar stands perhaps only with Alexander the Great and Genghis Khan.

But what distinguishes Caesar even from Alexander is Caesar's political and strategic sagacity. Alexander was the favored son; through his battlefield success he kept his armies unified and held together his logistics. And at the end, he failed politically and strategically. Caesar, on the other hand, started his life in politics, as a young man of a distinguished and wealthy but out-of-favor family. He had to maneuver his way to the top. And then, even while engaged in combat, battles, and campaigns on Rome's frontiers, he kept his footing in the slippery politics of Rome, first by forging strategic alliances, and then by, as a last resort, engaging in civil war against envious, jealous rivals. He was also a master of intrigue, intelligence collection, and strategic preemption against the plethora of barbarian and semi-civilized tribes in Roman provinces. He used bribery, intimidation, hostage taking, strategic assassination, scorched-earth tactics, and mass reprisals at the strategic level—much of which today is patently illegal and totally out-of-bounds for Western commanders. But Caesar's only standard was expeditious success, and, with few exceptions, he avoided personal sentimentality as well as legal or moral scruples. He was about power, and he used every tool and means at his disposal, including the vast personal wealth gained by his conquests, to achieve and maintain his growing power.

Caesar was the master of war and politics. But as much as his raw talents and skill can be admired, his career and achievements also pose a stark warning. He was the proverbial "man on horseback," much feared by the framers of our Constitution, someone whose reckless pursuit of self-interest through war ultimately destroyed the institutions of Republican Rome and paved the way for an empire driven by dictatorship, tyranny, and corruption. Hopefully, we will continue to be mindful of the lessons of his life, but won't see his like again.

—*General Wesley K. Clark (Ret.)*

I Came, I Saw, I Conquered

FRAMED AGAINST THE AUTUMN FOLIAGE ON THE RIDGES HIGH ABOVE the valley was an endless line of mounted riders. It was 52 BC in what is now eastern France, and the fierce-looking Gallic warriors with long, unkempt beards carried swords and axes and all manner of savage weapons. There were not merely hundreds of these men, nor even thousands, but tens of thousands. Some historians even put the number at a quarter of a million.

In the center of the valley was Alesia, a fortified city where Vercingetorix, the greatest Gallic warlord and the first leader to have united his countrymen, watched and waited. He meant to resist this foreigner from across the Alps who had dared to think so big as to subjugate all Gaul under one rule. Indeed, no leader from within Gaul had ever dared to conceive of something so politically far reaching. Vercingetorix had unified only the Gauls' armies, and only as a means of resisting this outsider, this Roman, this man named Gaius Julius Caesar.

During the preceding weeks Caesar had surrounded Vercingetorix in Alesia and was about to initiate a clash of civilizations to decide who would be the master of Gaul. The Gallic clarion had called out to all the lands, summoning all the armies of all the tribes to help Vercingetorix crush Caesar. They had answered that call.

Caesar himself was now surrounded by the countless warriors on the ridges above the valley. He had tens of thousands of warriors, a dozen Roman legions, but for each of his men there were five or six Gauls.

It promised to be the largest, bloodiest, most horrible battle ever seen in northern Europe.

The two armies had skirmished for several days, but at last the time for climactic struggle had come. The great horde swept down from the hills like a tidal wave, surging against and over the Roman defensive lines and the Roman defenders themselves. The Gauls created a breach in the Roman line and surged through.

Suddenly, Julius Caesar appeared amid his battling troops.

"Do not succumb to this travail," he exhorted them. "The fruits of all former engagements depend on this day and on this hour."

They had been victorious in many battles across Gaul in the preceding six years, but all now came down to what would happen in the next hour.

Caesar countered the Gallic tsunami with a wave of Roman troops from elsewhere in his lines, flooding the breach with 6,000 more men. He then personally led a mixed infantry and cavalry contingent in counterattack against the mass of Gallic warriors hammering the Roman lines.

It was a brazen move, the kind no prudent commander would make, because the risks far outweighed any chance of success. The tactic was that of either a desperate leader or a leader with supreme confidence in the bravery of his men and his own skill.

Suddenly, Caesar and his gallant cavalry had outflanked their enemy and were at his rear. The Gallic assault sputtered first to a halt, then into confusion and panic. The Gauls stumbled over one another to retreat as fast as they could.

Seeing this, the besieged Roman troops within the defensive lines, who moments before had been fighting for their lives, gave chase. As the Gauls fled through the woods, the Romans chased them like demons, hacking them to pieces if they slowed their pace.

Julius Caesar's victory at Alesia marked an end to the Gallic resistance against Roman rule and permanently enshrined Caesar's reputation as a conquering hero. Though not all his later victories came easy, Caesar often gave the impression that they were effortless. One response in particular is memorable. After his defeat of Pharnaces at Zela in 47 BC, Caesar simply shrugged and said, "Veni, vidi, vici"— I came, I saw, I conquered.

This phrase became truly immortal, one of the most memorable in military history and one that clearly encapsulates the world's most celebrated military leader in the two millennia between Alexander the Great and Napoleon Bonaparte. Like them, Caesar was the standard by which all military leaders of his era were measured, and he still ranks among the generals most studied by military professionals.

Julius Caesar was also one of the first great military leaders to lead a parallel life as a military historian. He wrote *Commentarii de Bello Gallico* (*Commentaries on the Gallic War*) and *Commentarii de Bello Civili* (*Commentaries on the Civil War*) when his two major campaigns were still fresh in his mind. They are thought to be based on his dispatches from the front, which were issued, almost like press releases, at the time of the actual campaigns. Despite this opportunity for self-congratulation, Caesar the historian was able to distance himself from Caesar the general, and he achieved a good measure of analytical objectivity. Caesar often is critical of, and willing to admit, his own tactical errors. This makes the works valuable both as a combat chronicle and as an insight into Caesar's tactical and strategic thinking.

His work is studded with insights useful to tacticians from any age. Among the better known is his assertion that "in bello parvis momentis magni casus intercedunt" (in war, events of importance are the result of trivial causes).

I quote both sets of commentaries often in these pages. In the chapters concerning his Gallic Wars, particular comments that I attribute to Caesar come straight out of *Commentarii de Bello Gallico*. Likewise, in the chapters concerning the civil war, quotes from Caesar are from *Commentarii de Bello Civili*. The specific translations are listed in the notes on sources at the end of this book.

Over time Caesar's biographers have become so entwined in his story that they emerge as characters within it. Two such men wrote the earliest biographies of him. Lucius Mestrius Plutarchus, better known as Plutarch, included Caesar in his first-century work *Lives of Noble Greeks and Romans*. Also in the first century Gaius Suetonius Tranquillus wrote the biography *Vita Divi Iuli* (*The Life of the Deified Julius*) as part of his 12-volume *De Vita Caesarum* (*On the Life of the Caesars*). Quotes from the biographies by Plutarch and Suetonius are accompanied by mention of their names. Full details of the specific translations I used appear in the notes on sources.

Julius Caesar was a complex man whose life was as filled by political intrigue as it was with military accomplishment. Even as I focus upon the latter here, I cannot ignore the former, as it was through his command of troops that he influenced Roman politics and later came to seize political power. He became the most influential figure in Roman history.

But it was as a general that Caesar pioneered the force structure and battle tactics by which future Roman generals would later expand the boundaries of the empire. He set the course of Roman rule for half a millennium, extended the Roman Empire from the Mediterranean to the North Sea, and defined the course of history, not merely of Rome, but of Europe as a whole.

CHAPTER 1

Roman Military History
before Caesar

THE ROME INTO WHICH JULIUS CAESAR WAS BORN IN 100 BC WAS the superpower of the Western world. Culturally, it was the most important civilization to exist in that world since Greece reached its cultural apogee during the golden age of Athens in the fifth century BC, and the most important military superpower since Alexander the Great had crushed the power of the Persian Empire in the fourth century BC.

Unquestionably, Rome was a legendary city. Indeed, the city was born of legend, beginning in the eighth century BC with a pair of twins named Romulus and Remus who are said to have founded the city. Whether the twins actually existed is not known, though archeological remains on the Palatine Hill, overlooking the Forum in the heart of what would become the city of Rome, indicate that an early settlement did exist there at that time. However, whether the twins actually existed is irrelevant. The Romans of Caesar's time, and for many centuries before and after, believed that the twins had, and their existence was a keystone of classical Rome's sense of time and place.

The mother of the twins was, according to legend, Rhea Silvia, a descendant of the Trojan prince Aeneas. She was the daughter of Numitor, the king of an ancient city-state in the Alban Hills about 15 miles southeast of Rome. As the legend goes, the father of the twins may have been the war god Mars or the heroic demigod Hercules. In ancient Greco-Roman legends it was not uncommon for a family to claim descent from a patriarch of such status. As with many ancient tribes around the world, the Romans had come to think of themselves as people descended from a deified mother. In the case of the Romans, especially certain Roman gentes, or families descended from a common ancestor, she was an aspect of the goddess Venus, called Venus Genetrix, or Mother Venus. Indeed, Julius Caesar's family, the gens Julia, was such a family. It believed itself to be descended from the mythological Ascanius (also called Iulius).

When Numitor was deposed by his brother, Amulius, Rhea was enslaved and the twins were left in the woods to die. However, they were suckled by a female wolf, discovered by a shepherd, and raised to manhood. In turn, Romulus and Remus killed Amulius, restored Numitor to his throne, and decided to build a new city. According to Plutarch, Remus was killed as the twins squabbled about its location, and Romulus established his city on the Palatine Hill. If the origin is the stuff of legend, the rest is, as they say, history.

Rome emerged early as an aggressive and acquisitive military power, destined to become the superpower of the Mediterranean. Rome soon became the most important power in central Italy, and later all of southern Italy as well. By the sixth century BC the Romans had conquered and subjugated the Etruscan civilization, as well as the civilizations of the Sabines and the Samnites.

Romans pioneered democracy, replacing their monarchy with a constitutional republican form of government at about the time that Athens was becoming a representative democracy. Caesar was born into the Roman Republic, which is said to date from 509 BC, although before that Rome had a powerful senate and the king was elected, albeit to a life term. The government of the Roman Republic was officially called Senatus Populusque Romanus (Senate and People of Rome, abbreviated as SPQR), indicating that true national sovereignty resided in Roman citizens, not in a king or leader.

Victory over Carthage in the First Punic War in 241 BC brought the first two provinces outside the Italian peninsula, Sicily and Sardinia, into the Roman Republic. Parts of the Iberian Peninsula followed, and at the beginning of the second century the Romans got involved in the affairs of the Greek world. By then all Hellenistic kingdoms and the Greek city-states were in decline, exhausted from endless civil wars and relying on mercenary troops. (The Battle of Corinth in 146 BC cemented the Greeks' fall and resulted in the establishment of Roman control over Greece.) Militarily, the politically sophisticated Roman Republic continued to expand its domain, until, by the third century BC, the Romans controlled all of Italy south of the Po River valley. North of this lay what the Romans called Gallia Cisalpina, or Cisalpine Gaul. In the Pyrrhic War of 280–275 BC the Romans defeated the former Greek colonies in Italy and Sicily, except Syracuse, and then absorbed them.

For all its success in land warfare, Rome had virtually no naval warfare experience and was therefore reaching the limits of its potential for expansion. The dominant naval power in the Mediterranean at this time—indeed, the preeminent Mediterranean superpower before Rome—was Carthage. This empire had originated in the ninth century BC as a Phoenician colony in North Africa based near modern-day Tunis. Of course, the Phoenicians had been the dominant maritime presence in the Mediterranean for centuries. Carthage was not only a naval power; it also had a land empire that comprised the coastline of North Africa and what is now southern Spain, as well as the islands of the western Mediterranean, including Sardinia, Corsica, the Balearic Islands, and much of Sicily.

As the Mediterranean superpower of the third century BC, Carthage would not go unchallenged by the ambitious Romans. This inevitable contest would occur over more than a century in the three major campaigns between 264 and 146 BC that are known as the Punic Wars.

The first of the three Punic Wars began with a Roman invasion of northern Sicily in 264 that resulted in the capture of the key

Carthaginian fortress city of Agrigentum in 262. At that point Rome finally decided to build a navy. By copying Carthaginian shipbuilding techniques, and introducing some design innovations of their own, the Romans built a fleet that won the Mediterranean naval battles of Mylae, near Messina in Sicily, and Cape Ecnomus, on Sicily's south coast. The latter paved the way for a seaborne Roman invasion of North Africa that threatened the Carthaginian capital itself. However, the campaign ended in a resounding Roman defeat in the spring of 255 BC.

Having realized that they had overextended themselves by taking the war to North Africa, the Romans next concentrated on attempts to expand their control of Sicily. However, Roman land victories in Sicily were offset by Carthaginian successes in the Mediterranean, culminating with a major Roman defeat in the naval Battle of Drepana in 249 BC. This battle resulted in a near total loss of the Roman fleet and an apparent decision by Rome not to rebuild it. In 244, after five years of going unchallenged at sea by the Romans, Carthage naturally assumed the war was over and began a general demobilization of its own fleet as a cost-cutting measure. However, the Romans used this opportunity to rebuild their navy, and in 241 they achieved a decisive naval victory in the Battle of the Aegates Islands. This really did end the First Punic War—with Rome as the victor. Rome now controlled all of Sicily except independent Syracuse, and Carthage no longer held naval supremacy in the Mediterranean.

The Second Punic War began in 218 BC as a dispute about Saguntum, a Mediterranean coastal city in what is now Spain (called Hispania by the Romans) that had ties to Rome. The prominent Carthaginian general Hannibal captured it and used it as the jumping-off point for his famous attempt to conquer Rome by land through a march over the Mediterranean coast of Europe and across the Alps. Hannibal's bold move in crossing the Alps to invade Italy and threaten Rome itself caused Rome to shelve a plan to bring the war to a fast conclusion by once again invading North Africa near Carthage. It would remain on the shelf for more than 15 years.

Hannibal managed to get across the Alps with more than 30,000 troops and three dozen elephants. Though he never reached the city of Rome, he did manage to defeat Roman armies east of Rome in the battles of Trebia in 218 BC and Lake Trasimenus in 217, and decisively at Canae in 216. Hannibal's biggest success was establishing a Carthaginian presence within Italy and causing several Italian cities to switch their allegiance from Rome to Carthage. Hannibal was also able to enlist support against the Romans from across the Adriatic in Macedonia, the ancestral home of Alexander the Great. Hannibal's incursion reached its high-water mark in 212 when Tarentum, the biggest Greek city in Italy, joined his coalition. For the moment he appeared invincible, having broken Rome's hegemony in its own backyard.

The Romans met Hannibal tactically on Italian battlefields, but their big-picture strategy involved hitting the Carthaginians farther afield, a strategic paradigm that would be revisited by Julius Caesar many years later. The brothers Scipio, renowned Roman generals, led a flanking action aimed at hitting the Carthaginian rear in Iberia. Though they failed to decisively defeat the Carthaginians, the Scipio brothers were able to bring the Kingdom of Numidia into the war on the Roman side. This ethnically Berber kingdom, which corresponds roughly to modern Algeria, had long been allied with and dependent upon Carthage. By seducing the Numidians away from their traditional loyalties, the Scipios opened up a new front in Africa, Carthage's home turf.

When both Scipio brothers were killed in 211 BC in Iberia, Publius Cornelius Scipio, the son of one of the brothers, led a Roman force to the region. After capturing Cartegena (New Carthage), the center of Carthaginian power in Iberia, in 209, he went on to win a series of important actions against the Carthaginians, including the Battle of Baecula (208 BC) and the Battle of Ilipa (206 BC). When Publius Cornelius Scipio was finished, so too was the centuries-old Carthaginian rule in Iberia.

By now Hannibal's luck was also running out, and the Carthaginian hold on parts of Italy was beginning to unravel. The Romans retook Tarentum in 209 and began to slowly roll back Hannibal's gains.

Meanwhile, the Romans dusted off the long-shelved plans for direct action against the city of Carthage itself. With Scipio in command they landed in North Africa at Utica in 203 and defeated the Carthaginian army in the Battle of the Great Plains. With this the Carthaginian government negotiated a peace treaty that might have ended the war. Essentially, it called for hostilities to end without either side relinquishing territory that it had occupied. Carthage would be allowed to keep its dominions in North Africa while officially ceding all the territory in Europe and the Mediterranean islands, including Sicily, Sardinia, and Corsica, that it had already lost to the Romans.

In the meantime, after almost 15 years in Italy, Hannibal had been recalled to Carthage to direct the defense of his homeland against the Romans. When the great hero of the war arrived home, many Carthaginians who had accepted the ceasefire were reenergized and resumed the fight. When Carthaginians sacked some Roman ships, the treaty, by now ratified by the Roman Senate, was rendered moot.

The climax of the Second Punic War came in October 202 in the desert at Zama, south of modern Tunis, with Hannibal leading an army of about 50,000—plus his signature war elephants—and Scipio an army of about 40,000.

The Battle of Zama went back and forth, but finally Scipio took and held the initiative. Hannibal went down in defeat, and Carthage was forced to accept a treaty with far harsher terms than the one it had abrogated. The Romans demanded reparations, required the Carthaginian army to disband, and limited the navy to a few ships for antipiracy patrols. For his great and final victory, Scipio was called Scipio Africanus.

In looking at the military history of Rome before Julius Caesar, historians tend to concentrate on the Punic Wars and the grand struggle between Rome and Carthage for control of the western Mediterranean. For the half century following the Second Punic War, as Carthage dutifully paid its reparations, Rome sought to pacify its newly won Iberian and Mediterranean island dominions— and looked eastward to the Adriatic Rim.

Italy sits on the western shore of the slender Adriatic Sea. On the opposite shore were a number of organized and disorganized states with limited military power, all generally unfriendly to Rome. In the north, roughly in the area now known as the "former Yugoslavia," was a place the Romans called Illyria, or Illyricum. Just as Yugoslavia was an amalgam of ethnically and linguistically unrelated populations, so too was the generally disunified Illyria. Some groups had become Roman subjects, while others sanctioned pirate fleets that harassed Roman shipping on the Adriatic.

Farther south, on the eastern part of the Adriatic Rim, lay Macedonia, the empire built to greatness in the fourth century BC by Philip II and maintained by his son Alexander the Great. As it had since the time of Philip, Macedonia's sphere of influence extended throughout Greece and the rim of the Aegean Sea. Unlike Illyria, which posed no serious conventional military threat, Macedonia was a military power to be reckoned with.

During the Second Punic War, when Hannibal occupied much of eastern Italy along the Adriatic Rim, Philip V of Macedonia spotted an opportunity and allied himself with Hannibal. Philip's contribution to the alliance consisted mainly of harassment of Roman shipping, and Rome took limited action to combat this. Meanwhile, Rome reinforced friendly enclaves and cultivated friendships and alliances with anti-Macedonian entities. These alliances gave Rome the pretext for a major war against the Macedonians.

After the conclusion of the second war with Carthage, Rome launched major operations against Macedonia in 200 BC. Rome's justification for this attack was that it was intervening to aid the Greek people who were being repressed by the Macedonians. The decisive Roman victory came in 197 BC with the Battle of Cynoscephalae. Thereafter, Philip V surrendered Macedonia to Rome as a client state, agreeing to pay reparations and never to conduct military operations outside his country. This marked the end of the era of Macedonian power that had begun with the father of Alexander the Great.

Parenthetically, the wars with Macedonia proved the tactical superiority of the versatile and adaptable Roman legion over the rigid phalanx organization that had served the Macedonians so well against the Persians and that had taken an invincible Alexander to the ends of the earth.

With the defeat of Macedonia, Rome's influence extended one sea farther east, from the Adriatic Rim to the Aegean Rim. This in turn brought the Romans on the western side of the Aegean face to face with the Seleucid Empire in Asia Minor (now Turkey). Another remnant of the once vast empire of Alexander the Great, the Seleucid

Empire had long been an important center of Hellenistic culture that incorporated most of what today is the Middle East, from Turkey through Syria and Iraq to Iran and beyond.

Having successfully eliminated Seleucid enclaves in Greece, the Romans took the fight into Asia Minor, where Scipio Africanus decisively defeated the army of Antiochus III the Great in the Battle of Magnesia in 190 BC. The subsequent Treaty of Apamea in 188 BC forced the Seleucids to pay reparations to the Romans and to give up Asia Minor.

With Rome's total dominance in the Mediterranean by the middle of the second century BC, that there should have been a Third Punic War seems counterintuitive but it happened. Among other provisions, the agreement that had ended the Second Punic War called for finite reparations to be paid by Carthage, and this tab was finally paid off in 151 BC. After half a century of kowtowing as the people of a Roman vassal state, the Carthaginians felt that all their obligations had now been met and that they were free to move on.

Rome disagreed and declared war in 149 BC. The Carthaginians could do little to resist a Roman invasion but pull into their fortified capital. The besieged city of Carthage finally fell three years later, whereupon the Romans sold the starving survivors into slavery and burned the city. The Romans sought to destroy Carthage stone by stone so as to erase its existence from the face of the earth, although stories that they salted the ground to prevent anything from growing were probably invented in later years.

After Carthage ceased to exist, Rome absorbed all its territories and client state relationships in the Mediterranean. The military history of Rome for the remainder of the second century BC would be dominated by efforts to compel obedience and subservience from these places and from other Roman territories.

In 135 BC, and again in 104 BC, Roman troops were called upon to put down major slave revolts in Sicily, leading to a series of conflicts known as the Servile Wars. The revolt in 73–71 BC led by the gladiator Spartacus, which has been embellished by modern popular culture, is also listed among the Servile Wars. Meanwhile, between 113 and 101 BC the Romans found themselves battling Germanic tribes from northern Europe in the Cimbrian War.

As the second century BC came to a close, Rome was in its ascendancy as a world power. In the century that followed the close of the Second Punic War, Rome had consolidated its power in the west and had expanded its influence eastward into the Middle East. Within the boundaries of the lands that Rome controlled and dominated, its legions had met and crushed all comers.

Less than two decades after crushing Carthage to dominate the western Mediterranean, Rome now dominated the eastern Mediterranean as well. The Romans were now the *only* Mediterranean power.

Meanwhile, at home the Romans had developed a complex constitution embodying such principles as separation of powers, and checks and balances. The thoughtful complexity of the republic's political institutions set Rome apart from most of the world known to Romans and their subjects. Rome had a written constitution that dated to the fifth century BC, and from this had flowed a legal system comprised of written laws enacted by an elected legislature.

Romans borrowed from Athens to develop an educational system unparalleled among major world centers. Technologically, the Roman road and aqueduct systems were soon to be built to an extent, and with a sophistication, that would not be matched by another Western civilization for centuries. In Roman cities, especially Rome itself, Romans walked on paved streets, and the upper classes lived in heated homes built of marble and served by indoor plumbing. Outside Rome, Romans traveled on paved roads at a time when most of the world traveled on narrow trails hardly more sophisticated than they had been a thousand years earlier. Romans charted the course of days with a calendar and the course of hours with water clocks. Like the Greeks during the golden age of Athens in the fifth century BC, Romans not only had a written language but a high level of literacy. In turn, this high level of literacy led to the flourishing of great literature, from philosophy to drama and from scientific studies to history. Many of the histories are still in print today, and several were sources for this book.

Julius Caesar was born into this superpower, with its complex society, at the turn of the first century BC. It was an auspicious moment for a man destined for greatness.

CHAPTER 2

Formative Years

GAIUS JULIUS CAESAR IS GENERALLY BELIEVED TO HAVE BEEN BORN ON July 13 in 100 BC in Subura, a working-class neighborhood in a valley west of the Esquiline Hill on the east side of Rome near where the famous Roman Coliseum was later built.

His father, also named Gaius Julius Caesar, was a 40-year-old Roman senator who had served as proconsul, or provincial governor, of the Roman province of Asia (now western Turkey). A member of the patrician upper class, the senator was the son and grandson of men also named Gaius Julius Caesar. Our Gaius Julius Caesar was the fourth generation in his family to bear the name. In Roman times the letters *J* and *U,* and all lowercase letters, did not exist, so the proper Latin spelling would have been GAIVS IVLIVS CAESAR, although GAIVS was also spelled as CAIVS.

The family were the IVLII, or Julii (plural of Julia), who arrived in Rome in the seventh century from the Alban Hills, which was coincidentally the origin of the mythical Romulus and Remus. The name Julii is derived from that of the family's legendary patriarch,

Iulus, also called Ascanius, who was the son of the mythical Aeneas. The claim by the founding brothers of Rome to descent from the mythical Aeneas would make all the Julius Caesars distant mythological cousins of Romulus and Remus.

More important than the family connection with a mere hero such as Aeneas was the belief of the Julii that they were direct descendants of the goddess Venus. While all Romans imagined such a connection with her, the Julii held festivals to celebrate Venus as their own special mother.

The source of the name Caesar is unclear and is often associated with birth by Caesarian section, because it seems to be derived from the verb *caedere,* meaning to cut down or to kill. The procedure was performed in Roman times in the case of a pregnant woman whose life could not be saved. There is no record that the first Gaius Julius Caesar was born this way, and our Julius Caesar almost certainly was not delivered by Ceasarian, as his mother lived for several decades after his birth.

The mother of our Gaius Julius Caesar was 20-year-old Aurelia Cotta, who hailed from a family of consuls on both sides. This was significant because consul was the highest elected office in the Roman Republic, which was ruled by a pair of consuls acting as colleagues, for a one-year term. Three of Aurelia's half brothers also held that rank.

Aurelia and the third Julius Caesar had three children, of whom our Julius was the youngest and the only son. The daughters were named Julia Caesaris Major and Julia Caesaris Minor. Nothing is known about the former, so perhaps she died in infancy. The middle child, who was about a year old when Julius was born, later married into a noble family, had three children, and died when she was about 50.

Our Julius Caesar also had an aunt named Julia Caesaris (his father's sister), who was married to the powerful Roman statesman and former general Gaius Marius. He served a remarkable seven terms as a consul, first elected in 108 BC, and was an influence upon the early development of his nephew.

Personally, Caesar appears to have been an athletic, self-confident youth with a quick mind and a gift for oratory that he later developed into an important asset in the political arena. He was, it is believed, prone to epileptic seizures, though perhaps not until later in life. His biographers mention six specific incidents that occurred during his last decade.

Young Julius Caesar grew up in an era when Rome's foreign wars were distant, but internal political strife in and near the capital was quite real and present. Beginning when Julius was about nine years old, Rome experienced the Social Wars, so named after the Latin *socii*, meaning allies. The specific allies were nearby Italian city-states that had been loyal friends to Rome for a long time. The wars were quite bloody but ended, when Julius was about 12, with the granting to the city-states limited representation in the Roman government. Though the fighting did not affect young Julius directly, he was certainly aware that it was going on, and this would have had an effect on his perception of how warfare was occasionally an effective means of resolving disputes.

While the Social Wars dominated the news close to home, the principal foreign conflict during Julius's youth was the Mithridatic Wars. These wars were fought between Rome and Mithridates VI, who ruled the Kingdom of Pontus, which was roughly in the northeast quadrant of modern Turkey, bordered by the Euxine Sea (now the Black Sea). These wars involved Mithridates's launching offensives against Roman-controlled areas of Asia Minor and Greece, punctuated by a massacre of tens of thousands of Roman citizens in 88 BC. The Mithridatic Wars contributed to the rise of the Roman general and consul Lucius Cornelius Sulla, who emerged as a war hero by defeating Mithridates and forcing him out of Greece by 84 BC.

Sulla is important to this narrative in that he was also the archrival of Julius Caesar's uncle Gaius Marius, the seven-term consul. Both served in the Roman army during the Social Wars. Having such a powerful political and military man as a family member and role model brought young Julius close to the intricacies and intrigues of power politics during his formative years. Seeing what was possible from a position of power inspired his imagination and foreshadowed his own maneuvering as an adult in the halls of power.

The rivalry between Sulla and Gaius Marius was also part of the backdrop to young Caesar's political coming of age. More than simply rivals, Sulla and Marius were standard-bearers for opposing political perspectives. Sulla was among the Optimates, best described as elitists who favored rule by the best and brightest of the upper crust. They favored a concentration of power in the aristocratic Senate, rather than in the democratic lower house, the Assembly. Marius, like Julius Caesar and his father, was among the Populares. As the name suggests, they favored having the power of the republic flow from popular democracy. The leaders of both factions, however, were members of the same elite—senatorial, upper class.

The enmity between the rivals came to a head in 88 BC, when the factions loyal to each within the Senate and the Assembly split over which of the two should be appointed to lead an expeditionary force headed to Greece. This led to Sulla's illegally marching on Rome with his legions to initiate a civil war. This in turn forced Marius into exile, giving Sulla both the command of the Greece expedition and the platform from which he became a war hero.

While both rivals were out of town, Lucius Cornelius Cinna, a Marius supporter, and Gnaeus Octavius, a supporter of Sulla's, were elected as the consuls. In turn, they had a civil war of their own that left Octavius dead. With his supporter now in command of Rome, Marius returned to be elected to his seventh term as consul, but he died of natural causes not long after, in early 86 BC, at age 70. After Cinna was killed in a mutiny in 84 BC while trying to put down a revolt in Illyria, Sulla decided that the time was right for him to return to Rome. A second civil war between Sulla and the supporters of Marius and his son climaxed in November 82 BC in a bloody battle at Rome's Colline Gate. After this Sulla was declared dictator, a position that superseded the rule of the consuls. Under Roman law a dictator was appointed only for a brief term, not to exceed six months, in order to execute a specific task. Though Sulla remained as dictator longer than anyone to date, he did reinstate the consular system within a year, although he stayed on as a consul. During his dictatorship Sulla was brutal in executing those he perceived as enemies of the state, but at the same time he expanded the number of seats in the Senate and increased the number of Roman courts. He also institutionalized for the first time the *cursus honorum,* which definitively specified the succession and hierarchy of offices within Roman government.

While all this was unfolding around him, the teenaged Julius Caesar was experiencing some momentous events in his own life. In 85 BC, his father died unexpectedly, and a year later Julius was nominated by Lucius Cinna, shortly before his own death, to be the new high priest of Jupiter. Cinna apparently had an ulterior motive in all this—the marrying-off of his 12-year-old daughter to the promising Julius. Because a priest was required to marry a woman of patrician rank, Caesar had to break off a previously arranged pairing.

As Suetonius writes, "Having previously been nominated priest of Jupiter, he broke his engagement with Cossutia, a lady of only equestrian rank, but very wealthy, who had been betrothed to him before he assumed the gown of manhood, and married Cornelia, daughter of that Cinna who was four times consul."

Based on his willingness to forgo a handsome dowry from Cossutia's family, and the longevity of the marriage—it lasted until her death in childbirth 16 years later—clearly there was more to his relationship with Cornelia than a mere arranged marriage. In calculating dates it seems possible that she was pregnant before the wedding. Their only daughter, Julia Caesaris, is reckoned to have been born in 85 BC, the year of the marriage, or perhaps the previous year.

As the nephew of Marius and now the son-in-law of Cinna, Julius Caesar was obviously not among the favorites of Sulla. Because the dictator targeted his opposition with bloody purges, Julius Caesar was forced into hiding. His life was saved, according to Suetonius, through the intervention of many prominent Romans, especially Julius's maternal uncle.

As Suetonius writes, "Everyone knows that when Sulla had long held out against the most devoted and eminent men of his party who interceded for Caesar, and they obstinately persisted, he at last gave way and cried, either by divine inspiration or a shrewd forecast: 'Have your way and take him; only bear in mind that the man you are so eager to save will one day deal the death blow to the cause of the aristocracy, which you have joined with me in upholding; for in this Caesar there is more than one Marius.'"

Plutarch agrees that Sulla saw many qualities of the uncle in the boy, writing that when Sulla was deliberating about putting Caesar to death, "some said there was no reason for killing a mere boy like him, [but] he declared that they had no sense if they did not see in this boy many Mariuses."

Though Sulla grudgingly absolved him of the guilt by association through his being related to Marius and Cinna, and spared him an early death, Caesar was stripped of his inheritance and his briefly held priesthood. Although his dowry had been confiscated, he declined to divorce Cornelia.

Such was Julius Caesar's introduction to the world of Roman politics.

CHAPTER 3

A Young Man on the Move

NEXT CAME JULIUS CAESAR'S INTRODUCTION TO THE ROMAN ARMY.

History, down to modern times, is full of stories of young men at loose ends who join the army to get away from an untenable situation at home. So it was with Caesar. As a priest he would not have been eligible for the military, so being stripped of his priesthood auspiciously opened up a new career path that would ultimately define his life.

As Suetonius writes, Caesar's first assignment as a soldier was in the Roman province of Asia, site of his father's earlier proconsulship; Caesar served on the personal staff of the provincial governor.

On one of his first assignments Caesar was sent to Bithynia, a kingdom under Roman rule on the Black Sea, a short distance east of what today is Istanbul. There he successfully enlisted the use of the fleet of Nicomedes IV of Bithynia, a man who had been allied with the Romans during the First Mithridatic War a few years earlier. Caesar later served briefly under the governor of Cilicia, on the coast of southern Asia Minor, where Caesar took part in the ongoing Roman campaign against pirates.

Julius Caesar soon proved himself a hero. Suetonius mentions that among Caesar's earliest combat actions was the storming of fortifications at Mytilene on the island of Lesbos in the Aegean Sea. In that fight he saved the life of a fellow Roman. For this he was awarded the Civic Crown, a crown of oak leaves that was the second-highest Roman award for bravery.

Another story that attests to the fearlessness of Julius Caesar involves his being captured by pirates near the island of Pharmacussa in the Aegean. The event is a window into Caesar's growing and audacious arrogance, and Plutarch writes that "when the pirates demanded 20 talents for his ransom, he laughed at them for not knowing who their captive was, and of his own accord agreed to give them 50."

That was a lot of money for a young soldier; the willingness of authorities to pay for his release is a sign that the importance of his family in the Roman political and social hierarchy was still considerable.

While they were all waiting on Pharmacussa for the ransom money to be delivered, Caesar taunted his captors, telling them that one day he would track them down and kill them. The pirates had a good laugh at this, but the joke would later be on them.

Plutarch notes that after his ransom had been paid and Caesar had been set free, he

immediately manned vessels and put to sea from the harbor of Miletus against the robbers. He caught them, too, still lying at anchor off the island, and got most of them into his power. Their money he made his booty, but the men themselves he lodged in the prison at Pergamum, and then went in person to Junius, the governor of Asia, on the ground that it belonged to him, as praetor of the province, to punish the captives.... But since the praetor cast longing eyes on their money, which was no small sum, and kept saying that he would consider the case of the captives at his leisure, Caesar left him to his own devices, went to Pergamum, took the robbers out of prison, and crucified them all, just as he had often warned them on the island that he would do, when they thought he was joking.

More important to Julius Caesar's later career than his clash with the pirates was his decision, made around this time, to spend some time on the island of Rhodes with Apollonius Molon, the great Greek orator and rhetorician. A teacher of public speaking, Molon helped mold Caesar's skills in this area, skills that were as important as his tactical skills to his later effectiveness as a leader. The incident with the pirates demonstrated the extraordinary self-confidence of an intelligent and ambitious young man. Molon was able to help Caesar develop the skills to express these qualities verbally, and to use his innate brilliance and forcefulness to craft arguments that could sway others to his points of view. These skills would serve him well for the rest of his life and career. Molon also tutored Caesar's contemporary, Marcus Tullius Cicero, who was perhaps the greatest Roman orator and one of the most renowned in the history of the classical world.

After Caesar's archenemy, Lucius Cornelius Sulla, died in 78 BC, perhaps as a result of complications from a stomach ulcer, the 22-year-old Julius Caesar was able to step out of the provincial shadows and make his way in Rome again.

In Rome, Caesar was elected to a post as military tribune, a rank analogous to that of a modern colonel, just below that of a legate, the equivalent of a general. In this position, as Suetonius describes it, he "ardently supported the leaders in the attempt to reestablish the authority of the tribunes of the commons [plebeian tribunes, a political office], the extent of which Sulla had curtailed." As a Populare, Caesar would devote his political career to supporting the cause of the plebians within Roman government and society.

Caesar's biographers have little more to say about him until just after he turned 30. In 68–69 BC he experienced the deaths of both his aunt Julia (the widow of Gaius Marius) and his young wife, Cornelia, who died in childbirth. His eulogies, delivered at the two funerals, are said to have solidified his reputation as a gifted orator.

That same year he was also named to the post of quaestor of Hispania, comprised of today's France and Spain, which had been wrested from Carthage in the Punic Wars. As a quaestor Caesar served as a supervisor of financial affairs, roughly analogous to a comptroller or auditor. As a career step it was an entry-level political posting rather than an indication that Caesar imagined himself destined for a vocation in the world of finance.

While traveling in his province, he happened by a temple of Hercules in Gades (now Cadiz, Spain), in which he saw a statue of Alexander the Great, whom he idolized. Caesar was deeply affected, for he aspired to one day be a conqueror like his hero.

As he stared at Alexander, the 32-year-old Caesar realized that he was the same age Alexander had been when he died.

As Suetonius writes, Caesar "heaved a sigh,... as if out of patience with his own incapacity in having as yet done nothing noteworthy at a time of life when Alexander had already brought the world to his feet."

Plutarch adds an anecdote from the same period, recalling that "when [Caesar] was at leisure and was reading from the history of Alexander, he was lost in thought for a long time, and then burst into tears." When his friends asked why he was crying, Caesar replied, "Do you not think it is matter for sorrow that while Alexander, at my age, was already king of so many peoples, I have as yet achieved no brilliant success?"

Alexander had conquered most of the known world by age 32. Caesar was an accountant in a provincial backwater. Of course, Alexander was dead at 32. Caesar had many years left in which to match the record of the young Macedonian.

In 67 BC, after serving the fixed term of his assignment, the ambitious Julius Caesar was back in Rome.

There, one year after the death of his wife, Cornelia, he married Pompeia, the granddaughter of his old nemesis, Lucius Cornelius Sulla. It was probably a politically motivated union, as it represented Caesar's entrée into the upper tiers of the Roman political establishment. The marriage ended in divorce five years later, when she had an affair with the Populare politician Publius Clodius Pulcher, who was infamous around Rome for his voracious bisexual sexual appetites.

Meanwhile, Caesar continued to make his way through the bureaucracy, next appointed to the minor administrative post of aedile and later to a more senior magisterial job as praetor. In this career path he found himself more and more immersed in the intrigues of government.

In 65 BC, according to Suetonius, Caesar was rumored to have had a peripheral role in the ill-fated Catiline Conspiracy, an attempt by Lucius Sergius Catilina and others "not only to subvert the constitution, but to destroy the whole government and throw everything into confusion."

Suetonius does add that "whether or not Caesar secretly gave these men any countenance and help, is uncertain; but after they had been overwhelmingly convicted in the senate, and Cicero the consul asked each senator to give his opinion on the manner of their punishment, the rest, down to Caesar, urged that they be put to death."

What this demonstrates about Caesar is his willingness to play the game of politics, regardless of his convictions. Though the idea of stepping on colleagues in the exercise of political expediency may seem to be a step onto the dark side, it was, for Caesar, an acceptance of reality. Being on the winning side of a political battle meant gaining the favor of those who might prove to be essential in future political power struggles.

In 63 BC Caesar saw an opportunity for political advancement and entered an election campaign against the powerful senators Isauricus and Catulus. Suetonius writes that Caesar got into the match to present himself "to the people as a rival candidate." Though the office they sought was that of pontifex maximus, which literally means "great bridge builder," it was a bitter and dirty campaign with accusations of bribery and impropriety all around. Despite the seniority and political muscle of his opponents, Caesar won by a comfortable margin. In this job Caesar served as high priest of the College of Pontiffs, essentially as the chief of the Roman state religion.

As an up-and-coming politician Caesar was beginning to move within intrigues at the upper levels of Roman politics. He now first became entangled with the two men—long-time rival power brokers, former Sulla henchmen, and former consuls—who were to feature most prominently in his political future. The two were the wealthy and influential former general Marcus Licinius Crassus and the charismatic political and military leader Gnaeus Pompeius Magnus (Pompey the Great). The latter had achieved his official status of greatness as a hero in, among other military campaigns, the Mithridatic Wars and operations against pirates in the eastern Mediterranean.

As he learned politics, Caesar also learned about both the cost of politics and the need for fund-raising. With this in mind, he now sought to move in the same circles as Crassus, who is often considered to have been the richest man in Rome. The alliance with Crassus against Pompey originated in 61 BC when Caesar was offered the governorship of Hispania. To take the job the former accountant needed Crassus to help him settle up his accounts. As Plutarch describes it, "Since [Caesar] found it hard to arrange matters with his creditors, who obstructed his departure and were clamorous, he had recourse to Crassus, the richest of the Romans, who had need of Caesar's vigor and fire for his political campaign against Pompey.... And it was only after Crassus had met the demands of the most importunate and inexorable of these creditors and given surety for eight hundred and thirty talents, that Caesar could go out to his province."

Caesar was probably glad to get out of town. As much as he was committed to his own political future, he found the infighting exhausting. Plutarch relates a story of Caesar's passing through a small town in the Alps on his way to Hispania when some of his men started joking about whether politics existed even in this little place, asking, "Can it be that here too there are ambitious strifes for office, struggles for primacy, and mutual jealousies of powerful men?"

"I would rather be first here than second at Rome," Caesar replied grimly.

Back in Hispania he was able to briefly return to his military career, which had been interrupted nearly two decades earlier when he returned to Rome from Asia Minor. Caesar could now establish himself as a competent senior military leader by conquering the Celtic tribes of the northwest corner of the Iberian Peninsula, north of the boundaries of the two Roman provinces of Hispania Citerior and Ulterior.

As Plutarch reports, Caesar "overpowered them, and marched on as far as the outer sea [Atlantic Ocean], subduing their tribes which before were not obedient to Rome. After bringing the war to a successful close, he was equally happy in adjusting the problems of peace, by establishing concord between the cities, and particularly by healing the dissensions."

These campaigns were historically important on two counts. First, they were prototypical of the type of asymmetrical counter-insurgency campaigns that Caesar would fight in northern Europe through much of his middle combat career. Like most operations that the Roman army conducted on the frontiers, these were characterized by a well-armed and well-disciplined force in conflict with a guerrilla army with less-sophisticated weapons and tactics. Though the guerrillas had the advantage of knowing the terrain, their lack of organization prevented them from creating a unified opposition to the Romans. Thus the Romans were able to conquer and hold disputed ground, creating the dominions that would form the Roman Empire.

Second, his success propelled his political career to heights achieved by only a few Romans at that time.

Having subdued these areas, Julius Caesar prepared to march back to Rome.

His victories were eligible to be officially hailed as a Triumphus ('Triumph), that is, they could be formally celebrated by the Roman Senate as military achievements against foreign enemies. This would make Caesar eligible for the title of imperator, or commander. (Although imperator was an honorary title, it became the root of the later term *emperor*.) Now that he was being hailed as a potential imperator, Caesar decided he wanted to stand for the civilian office of consul, the republic's highest magisterial office.

However, the law did not allow a military officer to run for consul. As Plutarch explains it, "Those who sued for the privilege of a Triumphus must remain outside the city, while those who were candidates for the consulship must be present in the city.... Caesar was in a great dilemma... because he had reached home at the very time for the consular elections."

Caesar had to chose between remaining as a general and becoming an imperator—or resigning his commission to run for consul. An ambitious man, he chose the latter.

CHAPTER 4

Consul and Proconsul

JULIUS CAESAR RETURNED TO ROME AFTER VICTORIES IN HISPANIA that proved him a master of the military arts. Thereupon he promptly proved himself also as a master of the political arts as he worked to conciliate the two former generals and former consuls who were the most powerful politicians in Rome.

Plutarch writes that "as soon as [Caesar] entered the city he assumed a policy ... to reconcile Pompey [Gnaeus Pompeius Magnus] and his political ally, [Marcus Licinius] Crassus, the most influential men in the city.... These men Caesar brought together in friendship after their quarrel, and by concentrating their united strength upon himself, succeeded, before men were aware of it."

In the 59 BC election for two consular posts, both Crassus and Pompey threw the considerable weight of their support behind Caesar. The two other candidates in the race were Lucius Lucceius, a Populare, or man of the people, and Marcus Calpurnius Bibulus, the elitist, pronobility Optimate candidate. As Suetonius writes, "Caesar joined forces with the former, making a bargain with him that since Lucceius had less influence but more funds, he should in their common name promise largess to the electors from his own pocket. When this became known, the aristocracy authorized Bibulus to promise the same amount."

In other words, the nobility was afraid that if both Caesar and his Populare ally were elected, they would have too much power. Therefore they supported Bibulus, an Optimate, as a perceived counterbalance to Caesar. The maneuver worked, and Lucceius came in third in the race for the two seats, which were balanced between a Populare and an Optimate.

Technically, Caesar's colleague was his co-consul, Bibulus, but behind the scenes his colleagues were Crassus and Pompey. The three secretly formed a powerful and proactive alliance, which later historians would call the First Triumvirate (to distinguish it from a later, post-Caesar, Second Triumvirate), although the term was not used at the time. This power center would be the predominant political force in the Roman Republic for the next six years, until the death of Crassus.

The principal political opponents to the concept and fact of the triumvirate were the great orator Marcus Tullius Cicero, Marcus Porcius Cato (aka Cato the Younger). Both were senators, prominent among the Roman ruling elite, and still celebrated as important political philosophers. Cato was especially well known for his incorruptibility, his moral integrity and refusal to be bribed.

However, the triumvirate outmaneuvered its political opponents within the halls of power. Pompey went a step further than the political, bringing troops loyal to him into Rome.

When political maneuvering did not work, Pompey was not above sending in his goons to aid Caesar and Crassus. As Plutarch writes, Pompey "filled the forum with armed men and helped the people to enact Caesar's laws." The notion of armed thugs in the halls of government was traditionally off-putting to most Romans, but the popular support for Caesar at the time seems to have made this show of muscle acceptable.

As for Bibulus, Plutarch tells that he "shut himself up in his house and for the eight months remaining of his consulship did not appear in public, but issued edicts which were full of accusations and slanders against Pompey and Caesar."

As much as the 32-year-old Caesar had bemoaned his accomplishments as pale compared with Alexander's, the 41-year-old Caesar had reached the apogee of power and prestige within the Roman Republic.

To solidify the alliance with Caesar, Pompey, aged 47, took Caesar's attractive 24-year-old daughter, Julia, as his fourth wife in April 59 BC. This occurred even though she was betrothed to Servilius Caepio and was going to be married to him within a few days. Plutarch, who recorded this affair, adds that "to appease the wrath of Caepio, Pompey promised him his own daughter in marriage, although she was already engaged."

Meanwhile, Caesar himself took Calpurnia, the 16-year-old daughter of the prominent politician Lucius Calpurnius Piso Caesoninus, as his third (and last) wife. In turn, Caesar facilitated Piso's becoming a consul the following year. Plutarch tells that Cato "vehemently protested, and cried out that it was intolerable to have the supreme power prostituted by marriage alliances and to see men helping one another to powers and armies and provinces by means of women."

When Caesar's term as consul expired, the triumvirate remained, its power undiminished. As wealthy and influential former consuls, Pompey and Crassus were content for the moment to act as power brokers. For Caesar his consulship was merely another achievement. It was typical for a man's term as consul to be followed by one year as a proconsul, or provincial governor; the specific province signified the degree of prestige in the job. In Caesar's case, he and his two allies engineered an arrangement by which he received a five-year term, and not one but three important provinces.

Naturally, the opposition registered dismay at Caesar's getting such a deal. As Plutarch relates, "Cato, of course, tried to speak against these measures, but Caesar had him led off to prison.... [W]hen Cato walked off without a word and Caesar saw not only that the most influential men were displeased, but also that the populace, out of respect for Cato's virtue, were following him in silence and with downcast looks, he himself secretly asked one of the tribunes to take Cato out of arrest."

Julius Caesar's three provinces were contiguous, and were, from east to west, Illyricum (now the western Balkans); Cisalpine Gaul (now northern Italy), which literally means Gaul on this side of the

Alps; and Transalpine Gaul (now southern France), which means Gaul on the far side of the Alps.

Transalpine Gaul was also known as Narbonese Gaul, or Gallia Narbonensis, after Narbo Martius (now Narbonne, France), the principal Roman city within its borders. Informally, many referred to Transalpine Gaul as "the Province," or "our Province," and as such it is the root of the modern French term for the region, Provence.

The Romans had been in Transalpine Gaul for nearly 100 years, having intervened in 154 BC on behalf of the residents of the Greek enclave at Massilia (now Marseilles, France) who were being attacked by Gallic tribes from the north. Within a generation Romans had defeated the Arverni, formerly the most powerful tribe in central France, and the Allobroges, and had allied with the powerful Aedui (also spelled Haedui) tribe to the north of the border of Transalpine Gaul.

After establishing Narbo as a major center, the Romans built a road called the Via Domita that ran along the coast, all the way from Rome to Hispania by way of Narbo.

Along with his proconsulship of this area Caesar had the military command of four veteran Roman legions, a significant armed force. These included the Legiones VI, VIII, IX, and X. Legio X, which he had previously commanded in Hispania, was his favorite and the legion he considered to be his elite personal guard.

A legion was the basic building block of the Roman army from the time of the republic through the era of the Roman Empire. Gaius Marius can be credited with molding the legion concept into a well-trained, well-organized unit. In a series of reforms undertaken at the end of the second century BC, he formalized the structure, standardized training and equipment, and gave Rome a standing army manned by a class of professional soldiers. This highly disciplined force made the Roman army what it was and contributed to its unprecedented successes.

The forward-thinking Marius had arranged for such men to be well paid and granted retirement benefits in the form of land grants. Retirement benefits would subsequently be adopted as an important element in the planning for the American Continental Army during the Revolutionary War.

The Roman legion usually consisted of 4,000 to 5,000 fighting troops, depending on the situation. These legionnaires, or legionaries, were mostly infantrymen, with a small contingent of attached cavalry known as *equites*. Mainly, cavalry was attached to a group of legions as an auxiliary force.

The legion was about half the size of a modern military division, but it was organized in a similar fashion, with support troops integral to the legion. The Roman equivalent of the modern infantry company was the century. As the name suggests, *centuriae* may have originally been conceived as consisting of 100 men, though in practice they included fewer, usually about 80.

The equivalent to the modern battalion would have been the cohort, which was ideally comprised of six centuriae. In turn, about ten cohorts made up a legion. Tactically, cohorts could operate as independent units if the situation called for a small-unit action.

The auxiliary troops that were integral to each legion ranged from archers and javelin throwers to engineers and cavalrymen, as well as a military intelligence staff. Each legion also had its own dedicated supply train, consisting of pack mules, although legionaries carried their own personal equipment. Standard equipment included a helmet, rectangular shield, and *gladius,* or short sword. The last reflected Roman tactics that involved thrusting, rather than slashing, as would be done with a longer sword.

The javelin throwers carried a six-foot spear with a two-foot metal shank called a *pilum.* The role of the javelin throwers was to create breaks or disruptions in the enemy line, or phalanx, that could be exploited by a group of swordsmen.

The centuriae were commanded by a professional officer called a centurion, and the cohorts by a senior centurion. A legion would have had about 60 centurions. Depending on seniority, centurions were like modern captains and majors in their duties and command responsibilities. Above the centurion in the Roman military hierarchy were the tribunes, who were roughly analogous to a modern colonel and functioned as staff officers. The equivalent of a modern general officer was a *legate,* who would typically command a legion. He would have been a member of the aristocracy, of praetorian or senatorial rank in civilian life.

In command of four such legions, with their legati, tribunes, and centurions, Julius Caesar prepared to march northward through nearby Cisalpine Gaul and across the Alps into Transalpine Gaul.

Gaul 58–52 BC
General Locations of
Selected Gallic Tribes

Miles
0   100   200

BRITANNIA

Cantiaci (Cantii)

Thames R.

English Channel

Atlantic
Ocean

Armorica
(Brittany)

Veneti

ODariorītum

Unelli

Aulercei

Lexovii

Belloaci

Morini

Atrebates

Vermandui

Menapii

Eburones

Nervii

Remi

Suebi

Suebi

Suebi

Rhine River

Ubii

Aduatuci

Treviri

Ardennes

Moselle River

Meuse R.

Aisne R.

OBibrax

ONoviodunum

Suessones

Lingones

Leuci

GERMANIA

Vosges Mountains

Helvetii

The Alps

Sequani

Octodurus

CISALPINE GAUL

B E L G I C A

Oise R.

Seine
River

Marne R.

Parisii

Lutetia
(Paris)

Senones

Aedui

Bibracte

Alesia

Boii

Gergovia O

Arverni

CELTICA

Loire River

Averīcum

Bituriges

Bituriges

Santones

Pictones

Sotiates

Nitiobriges

Ausci

Aquitani

AQUITANIA

Cévennes

Rivern

Rivern

Allobroges

TRANSALPINE GAUL

O Narbo

O Massilia
(Marseilles)

Mediterranean Sea

CHAPTER 5

Victory at Bibracte

In March 58 BC, as Proconsul Julius Caesar looked north into Transalpine Gaul, it did not take a man of his strategic imagination to see the opportunities for conquest that lay across the border of the provinces that he now governed. This boundary had long been the limit of Rome's dominions. Across it lived Celtic peoples who had never been subjugated by Roman arms, nor seduced by the splendor of Roman civilization.

North of Transalpine Gaul lay the rest of unconquered Gaul (northern France, Belgium, and beyond). In his autobiographical *Commentarii de Bello Gallico* (*Commentaries on the Gallic War*) Caesar describes the region as being inhabited by people "who in their own language are called Celts, in ours, Gauls." With great over-simplification, he divides the Gauls north of Transalpine Gaul into three parts: Belgica, home of the tribes collectively known as Belgae (Belgians), who lived north and east of the Seine River; Aquitania, home of the Aquitani, in the area roughly contiguous with the

Aquitaine Region of France; and everyone in between, who were called Celtae (Celts).

The Celts included the people called Helvetii, who lived in the Alps east of the Rhone River and whose name is the root of Helvetia, the personification of modern Switzerland. Caesar noted that the Helvetii "surpass the rest of the Gauls in valor, as they contend with the Germans [across the Rhine] in almost daily battles, when they either repel them from their own territories, or themselves wage war on their frontiers.... There was no doubt that the Helvetii were the most powerful of the whole of Gaul."

Indeed, the Helvetii had inflicted an especially degrading defeat on a Roman force under the command of the former consul Longinus near Agendicum (near present-day Bordeaux) in 107 BC, killing Longinus and humiliating the captured Roman troops. Caesar was well aware of what had happened. The grandfather of Caesar's father-in-law was also killed in the battle.

Among the many other Celtic people who lived in the area of Gaul between the Belgae and the Aquitani were the Aedui, the dominant tribe in what is now south-central France. They had been Roman allies for 60 years by the time Caesar reached Transalpine Gaul. As had been the case for centuries, the people of Gaul north of the Roman provinces were in a continuous state of low-intensity intra-Gallic combat, characterized by raids and counterraids. Because the Aedui were long-time friends of the Romans' Caesar might have used this as an excuse for the opening gambit of his Gallic Wars.

However, even as Caesar headed north, the Helvetii were in the midst of a major migration that had started around 60 BC. The Helvetii were leaving the Swiss Alps to occupy what is now southeastern France, threatening Caesar's Transalpine Gaul. Conquering and occupying open country apparently was appealing to the Helvetii, who were traditionally confined to mountains and narrow valleys. As Caesar observed, the scheme was the brainchild of a leader named Orgetorix, who was "by far the most distinguished and wealthy" of the Helvetii. According to Caesar, he told his people that they should "go forth from their territories with all their possessions, that it would be very easy, since they excelled all in valor, to acquire the supremacy of the whole of Gaul."

Orgetorix then set out on an unauthorized secret mission to convince various Roman client states in the area to switch sides. Caesar reports that he cut a deal for an alliance with Casticus of the Sequani, as well as Dumnorix of the Aedui, who "at that time possessed the chief authority in the [Aeduan] state, and was exceedingly beloved by the people."

As Caesar notes, Orgetorix was generous in his promises, even going so far as to give his own daughter to Dumnorix. However, Orgetorix failed in his scheme to subvert the Gallic tribes through political maneuvering before he brought in his army. Because of the embarrassing failure of this intrigue, which was not widely popular at home in the first place, Orgetorix was arrested by his own people but apparently committed suicide before he could be formally condemned to death.

Despite this, the Helvetii decided to go ahead with the planned relocation in the spring of 58 BC. They gathered up their women and children, along with livestock and food supplies, and prepared to head west. They even burned their homes, towns, and granaries, so that they would not be tempted to give up and go back.

As they began the march, they were joined by several neighboring tribes that had crossed the Rhine to be part of this adventure. According to written census documents later recovered by Julius Caesar, 368,000 people were involved in this mass migration, including 263,000 Helvetii, 36,000 Tulingi, 32,000 Boii, 23,000 Rauraci, and 14,000 Latobrigi.

Unfortunately for the Helvetii and their friends, their timing coincided with Caesar's impending arrival in Transalpine Gaul. Equally unfortunate was their choice of a route for the migration. They might have gone directly, through the Jura Mountains north of Lake Geneva. It was technically difficult, but it would have taken them much farther to the north of the borders of Caesar's province, thus keeping them a considerable distance from his legions. Yet, as Caesar observes, on this road not taken "scarcely one wagon at a time could be led [and] there was, moreover, a very high mountain overhanging, so that a very few might easily intercept them."

Thus, the Helvetii instead chose to take an easier road that led through Transalpine Gaul, crossing the Rhone in the distant edge of the land of the Allobroges, a tribe that was loyal to Rome. To their credit the Helvetii sent word to Caesar requesting safe passage. His response that he would consider their request was merely a stalling tactic. He had only one legion with him, having garrisoned his other three in Cisalpine Gaul, and he needed time to move the others. He even went a step further by forming an additional two (Legio XI and Legio XII), a step that would give him a strength of six legions with which to deal with the Helvetii.

During April, as negotiations continued, and as Caesar was assembling his army, the Helvetii turned north and began battling their way through the lands of the Aedui. As Caesar writes, "The Helvetii had by this time led their forces through the narrow defile and the territories of the Sequani, and had arrived at the territories of the Aedui, and were ravaging their lands. The Aedui, as they could not defend themselves," appealed for Roman help.

Caesar's advanced recon contingent caught up with the Helvetii and quietly observed them as they were crossing the slow-moving Saône River in the southern part of what is now France's Burgundy Region. Because the Helvetii had brought their dependents and household goods as well as military supplies, rafting everything across was an arduous process that took several days.

Upon hearing this from his observers, Caesar hurried to the Saône with three legions, arriving as about 75 percent of the Helvetii contingent had made the crossing. He launched a swift surprise attack on the 25 percent of the Helvetii who were still south of the river. He notes that he "cut to pieces a great part of them [as] the rest betook themselves to flight, and concealed themselves in the nearest woods."

He later learned that the particular clan, or canton, of the Helvetii that he had defeated were the Tigurini, the same who had killed Lucius Cassius Longinus nearly half a century before. Caesar happily noted this coincidence in *Commentarii de Bello Gallico:* "By chance, or by the design of the immortal gods, that part of the Helvetian state which had brought a signal calamity upon the Roman people was the first to pay the penalty."

As soon as the battle was over, Caesar's engineers quickly built a bridge across the Saône. The majority of the Helvetii, who were already across, hurried to pick up and leave, hoping that they had a head start. However, although it had taken them as much as a week to get across, they were stunned to see that the Roman teams were able to build their pontoon bridge in just one day. It was not that the Romans were innately smarter or that they worked harder. They were able to build the bridge so quickly because Roman military doctrine stressed planning for important contingencies that might be met in the field. This was one of many instances when the superior organization, training, and technical skill of the Roman legions was manifest.

The Helvetii were forced to ponder their options and reopen negotiations. The Helvetii delegation was headed by an old warlord named Divico, whom Caesar recalls as having been in command during the Roman defeat at Agendicum.

"If the Roman people would make peace with the Helvetii, they would go to that part and there remain, where Caesar might appoint and desire them to be," said Divico in dialogue recalled by Caesar. In other words, he was proposing that if Caesar would grant the Helvetii territory in Gaul and appoint them as lords of that domain, they would cause him no further trouble. Divico opened with a conciliatory tone but continued in a taunting, almost threatening, manner: "But if he should persist in persecuting [us] with war, he ought to remember both the ancient disgrace of the Roman people and the characteristic valor of the Helvetii."

Referencing Caesar's having attacked the troops south of the river, when those on the north side could not come to their aid, Divico went on to deride the Romans for having learned "from their sires and ancestors [to] rely more on valor than on artifice and stratagem."

Caesar was incensed by Divico's "insolent boasting," replying that even if he were willing to forget the "former outrage" at Agendicum, he could not "also lay aside the remembrance of the late wrongs, in that they had against his will attempted a route through [Transalpine Gaul] by force," molesting the Aedui and the Allobroges. He then told Divico that he would allow them to retreat to a place of his choosing, but he would insist on their surrendering hostages as a guarantee.

Divico replied arrogantly that "the Helvetii had been so trained by their ancestors, that they were accustomed to receive, not to give, hostages; of that fact the Roman people were witness."

With this the old Helvetii leader returned to his side of the river. The negotiations were finished. The following day the Helvetii pulled out and headed north through the heartland of the Aedui.

Caesar decided not to attack but monitored the progress of the slow Helvetii wagon train and chose an ideal place to strike. For this he used a sizable cavalry contingent, which he reckons at about 4,000 strong, including Aedui and other Gallic horsemen. Heading the Aeduan cavalry was Dumnorix, who had earlier been seduced into considering a clandestine alliance with the Helvetii. This affair remained a secret, and Caesar was unaware of Dumnorix's questionable allegiance to his army.

Caesar's large cavalry force soon found itself in an unanticipated skirmish with the Helvetii. As Caesar notes, "Having too eagerly pursued the enemy's rear, [these troops] come to a battle with the cavalry of the Helvetii in a disadvantageous place, and a few of our men fell."

In turn, "the Helvetii, elated with this battle, because they had with five hundred horse repulsed so large a body of horse, began to face us more boldly, sometimes [also] from their rear to provoke our men by an attack."

However, Caesar restrained his men from battle, "deeming it sufficient for the present to prevent the enemy from [abuse and devastation]. They marched for about fifteen days in such a manner that there was not more than five or six miles between the enemy's rear and our van."

By now Caesar was becoming painfully aware of the problems of maintaining a huge field army in pursuit mode. He had depended upon barging food up the Saône to feed his troops, but as the Helvetii moved farther north of the river, this was more difficult. He bargained with the Aedui for corn with disappointing results. Promises were made, but they went unfulfilled. The grain was still ripening in the fields.

Worse, Caesar was now learning of the faction within the Aedui that was not loyal to Roman interests. Of Dumnorix, he writes that he is

a man of the highest daring, in great favor with the people on account of his liberality, a man eager for a revolution: that for a great many years he has been [exploiting and stealing from the Aedui, by which] he has both increased his own private property, and amassed great means for giving largesse; that he maintains constantly at his own expense and keeps about his own person a great number of cavalry, and that not only at home, but even among the neighboring states, he has great influence... that he has himself taken a wife [the daughter of Orgetorix] from among the Helvetii.

Caesar also determined, "on inquiring into the unsuccessful cavalry engagement which had taken place a few days before, that the commencement of that flight had been made by Dumnorix and his cavalry; that by their flight the rest of the cavalry were dismayed."

In turn, Caesar brought this information to Divitiacus, Dumnorix's brother and an Aedui leader still loyal to Rome. With tears in his eyes Divitiacus acknowledged to Caesar that "those charges are true, and that nobody suffered more pain on that account than he himself did... [but] if anything very severe from Caesar should befall [Dumnorix], no one would think that it had been done without his consent, since he himself held such a place in Caesar's friendship."

Finally, Caesar and Divitiacus agreed to put Dumnorix under surveillance so that they "may be able to know what he does, and with whom he communicates."

The same day as his exchange with Divitiacus, Caesar learned from his recon team that Divico and the Helvetii were camped just eight miles from his own camp at the foot of a gently sloping mountain. This, to Caesar's excitement, was exactly the sort of terrain he was waiting for to launch an attack on the slow-moving Helvetii.

The timing of the information was good in that the Roman troops were getting close to the end of their rations. Caesar was almost at the point where he would have to break off the pursuit and return to the Saône, where supply barges could reach him.

That night Caesar ordered his second in command, the legatus and professional soldier Titus Atius Labienus, to take the two newly formed legions and circle around to the top of the mountain under cover of darkness. They were to wait there until Caesar led the main attack, thereby ensuring that the Helvetii could be flanked and struck from two sides. Next, Caesar sent his entire cavalry contingent to approach the Helvetii along the same route that they had taken earlier.

By dawn, as the main Roman force approached to within two miles of the Helvetii camp, Caesar received erroneous information that Titus Labienus was not holding the high ground above the camp, and that the Helvetii were up there instead. By the time Caesar was able to sort things out, the Helvetii had broken camp and moved out of the trap that Caesar had tried to set.

Caesar was now in a tenuous situation. He had just suffered a tactical setback, although his enemy was not fully aware that it was about to be attacked. The Helvetii knew the Romans were nearby but not that they had just planned and canceled a major attempt at a decisive battle.

Caesar's biggest problem was that he was down to the critical point on rations for his six legions. Rather than looking back toward the Saône, he looked forward. The Romans were now just 18 miles from Bibracte, the well-provisioned principal city of the Aedui. Caesar would have to break off his close pursuit of the Helvetii, but if he could get his legions to Bibracte, at least they could eat.

When they saw the Romans divert toward Bibracte, the Helvetii were delighted, taking this tactical withdrawal as an opportunity to go on the offensive. Perhaps they knew that the Romans were making a dash for supplies and hoped to cut them off, or perhaps the Helvetii were merely seizing an opportunity to strike the rear guard of a retreating foe.

Fortunately for Caesar, the Helvetii attacked as the Roman column was heading up the slope of a hill. Therefore, when the enemy struck, Caesar's men had the high-ground advantage.

Caesar followed the conventional Roman tactical practice of holding one unit in reserve for each two that he put into the battle line. Placing Legio XI and Legio XII in reserve at the top of the hill, Caesar took command of a triple line of four infantry legions at the middle of the hill and sent his cavalry down and forward "to sustain the attack of the enemy."

The Helvetii repulsed the initial Roman cavalry attack, then formed into a phalanx and advanced uphill against the four legions.

The sizes of the respective forces are unknown, although rough estimates are possible. The four Roman legions would have numbered more than 20,000, with a cavalry contingent of 4,000, plus reserves of more than 10,000. Caesar later estimated the reserve of the Helvetii at 15,000, so their phalanx may have been double that number. Of course, Caesar's estimate of enemy strength is subject to exaggeration.

Hurling javelins from the high ground, the Romans broke the phalanx, then launched a counterattacking charge with swords drawn. The Romans found themselves fighting men who had discarded their shields. As Caesar described it, the javelins had pierced the shields, and they were "pinned fast together, as the point of the iron had bent itself [so] they could neither pluck it out, nor, with their left hand entangled, fight with sufficient ease [therefore] many, after having long tossed their arm about, chose rather to cast away the buckler from their hand, and to fight with their person unprotected."

After bloody hand-to-hand combat, the line of the Helvetii collapsed and they withdrew, pursued by Caesar's four veteran legions. As the Helvetii withdrew up the slope of an adjacent hill, their reserves, contingents of Boii and Tulingi that had been guarding the supply train, attempted to outflank the attacking Romans.

Caesar then turned a third of his command to face the estimated 15,000 men of the Helvetian reserve, while the other two-thirds maintained the pursuit of the main body of enemy that they had just chased from the other hill. This now was the main event of the Battle of Bibracte, which was, in Caesar's words, a "contest long and vigorously carried on with doubtful success. . . . For during the whole of this battle, although the fight lasted from [noon] to eventide, no one could see an enemy with his back turned."

As night fell, the Romans gained the upper hand, and the Helvetii withdrew, using the parked supply wagons for cover.

"The fight was carried on also at the baggage till late in the night," Caesar writes. "For they had set wagons in the way as a rampart, and from the higher ground kept throwing weapons upon our men, as they came on, and some from between the wagons and the wheels kept darting their lances and javelins from beneath, and wounding our men. After the fight had lasted some time, our men gained possession of their baggage and camp."

When it was over, Caesar was pleased to find among his prisoners the daughter and one of the sons of Orgetorix. Caesar also notes that 130,000 Helvetii escaped. They may have included some of the women, children, and other Helvetian civilian migrants who had left the Alps to settle on the plains of central France. It seems probable that they were not part of the battle force, because those numbers would have smothered Caesar's six legions had they been armed troops. Indeed, in a later calculation Caesar lists the total number of Helvetii capable of bearing arms before the losses in the battles of the Saône or Bibracte—and puts their number at 92,000.

Before giving chase, Caesar paused for three days to rest and feed his troops, care for his wounded, and bury those killed in action.

Within about a week he learned that the Helvetian stragglers from the Bibracte fight, however many there were, had marched north day and night for four days and had sought refuge in the land of the Lingones, another Celtic tribe that lived at the headwaters of the Seine and Marne Rivers in what is now France's Champagne-Ardenne Region. He then sent a message to the Lingones, telling them that the Roman legions were coming, and that if they aided the Helvetii in any way, he would consider them his enemies as well.

As he was marching north, Caesar met a delegation of Helvetii begging to surrender. In his own description, spun for Roman ears, he bragged that they had thrown themselves at his feet, and "speaking in suppliant tone had with tears sued for peace."

When he caught up to the main group of Helvetii, he ordered them to return to their original homes in the Alps—although he agreed to a request from the Aedui that the Boii be allowed to remain in central France.

Caesar's rationale in wanting the Helvetii back in the Alps was that he did not want to create a vacuum into which the Germanic tribes might be tempted to move. He would rather have the beaten Helvetii than the Germans living in the mountains that bordered both Cisalpine and Transalpine Gaul.

Having crushed the Helvetii and sent them home, Julius Caesar wrote, certainly with an eye for how the news would be received in Rome, that "ambassadors from almost all parts of Gaul," as well as chiefs and heads of state, assembled to congratulate him. He had, in his own view, done them all a huge favor. As he put it in *Commentarii de Bello Gallico,* this "circumstance had happened no less to the benefit of the land of Gaul than of the Roman people, because the Helvetii, while their affairs were most flourishing, had quitted their country with the design of making war upon the whole of Gaul, and seizing the government of it, and selecting, out of a great abundance, that spot for an abode."

Julius Caesar had come to Transalpine Gaul with thoughts of going north of its border for the purpose of conquest, but instead he had wound up fighting an unanticipated defensive campaign against a mass migration. However, it had all worked out quite well for the proconsul's grand plan for himself. He had been handed an opportunity not only to achieve a powerful victory but to drive his foe out of the land. He had gained his greatest military success to date, but by defeating Divico he had done even more. He had exacted vengeance for the embarrassing, festering wound of humiliation and death of Lucius Cassius Longinus 50 years before.

This had to have played well for Julius Caesar's reputation back home.

CHAPTER 6

Wild and Savage Men

WHEN JULIUS CAESAR DEFEATED THE HELVETII IN 58 BC, AND THE "ambassadors from almost all parts of Gaul" came to greet him, he was able to tell his fans in Rome that the ambassadors had done so to congratulate him and to celebrate his having removed a mutual enemy. However, they had more on their agenda than this. The reality was that Caesar had established a powerful military presence in Gaul, and the leaders felt it best to curry favor with the charismatic leader.

Some, who met with Caesar privately afterward, used the opportunity to seek his aid as a protector in intra-Gallic rivalries. Among these, his friend Divitiacus of the Aedui took him aside to complain about a problem that the Aedui were having with their old nemesis, the Arverni, of what is now France's Auvergne Region.

The Arverni were the military and political powerhouse of central France until they had been crushed by the Romans 65 years earlier, and the Arverni had been an annoyance to the Aedui for as long as anyone could remember. Under their alliance with the Romans, the Aedui had been able to deal with this, but the situation had changed. The Arverni, as well as the Sequani, were getting help from the warlike German tribes east of the Rhine. Indeed, as Caesar knew, the Aedui had lost a major battle with the Germani at Magetobria (near modern Luxeuil) in 63 BC.

Greater Germany, or Germania Magna in Latin, was generally defined by the Romans as the land east of the Rhine and north of the Alps that was occupied by various Germanic tribes, especially the powerful Suebi. The Romans imagined the Germani to be more barbaric and uncivilized than the Gauls and hence a more dangerous and more feared foe.

As Divitiacus and Caesar discussed, about 15,000 Germani had crossed the Rhine over the previous several years, and, like the Helvetii, had found the place much to their liking and sent word back to their cousins in Germania. As Caesar writes of the Germani in *Commentarii de Bello Gallico*, after they crossed the Rhine,

> these wild and savage men had become enamored of the lands and the refinement and the abundance of the Gauls, more were brought over, that there were now as many as 120,000 of them in Gaul: that with these the Aedui and their dependents had repeatedly struggled in arms…that they had been routed, and had sustained a great calamity…had lost all their nobility, all their senate, all their cavalry. And that broken by such engagements and calamities, although they [the Aedui] had formerly been very powerful in Gaul, both from their own valor and from the Roman people's hospitality and friendship, they were now compelled to give the chief nobles of their state, as hostages.

It was well known by this time that the leader of these "wild and savage men [who] had become enamored" with the Gallic life was the Germani warlord known in Latin as Ariovistus. (Various scholars have tried without success to determine his name in German.) During Caesar's consulship Ariovistus had sent conciliatory emissaries to Rome seeking friendship, and he had been recognized as a "king and friend" by the Roman senate two years earlier.

As for his being a "friend" to Roman interests, Ariovistus was clearly of the "fair weather" variety. As for his being a king, he needed a Roman senatorial proclamation to confirm it. He was the unquestioned leader, not only of the Suebi but of other allied Germanic tribes as well. In this role he had led the Germani in the defeat of the Aedui at Magetobria. (The tribal name *Suebi* is considered to be the etymological source for the name of the southwestern German region now known as Swabia.)

Subsequent to being named a friend of Rome, Ariovistus had come to Gaul to stay. He had even married a Gallic noblewoman as one of his two wives. By taking up residence in what is now the Alsace Region of France, Ariovistus and his people were seeding centuries of territorial disputes in the area. In the nineteenth and twentieth centuries, for example, the region was disputed by the French and the Germans, changing hands several times from the Franco-Prussian War of the 1870s through the two world wars of the twentieth century.

It angered Divitiacus that Ariovistus had settled in a third of the Aedui territory. Divitiacus must have been even more angry that in the summer of 58 BC, Ariovistus had, as Caesar writes, ordered the Aedui "to depart from another third part"—Ariovistus had recently invited to the area 24,000 Harudes from what is now Denmark, having promised them homes in the lands of the Aedui. As Caesar writes, the Aedui now had good reason to believe that "in a few years they would all be driven from the territories of Gaul, and all the Germani would cross the Rhine."

As Divitiacus probably put it to Caesar, he had ridded Gaul of the Helvetii, but what about the Germani swarming into Gaul?

Caesar told the Aeduan leader that "this affair should be an object of concern," adding that he had great hopes that both by Roman kindness and Roman power he could induce Ariovistus to put an end to his oppression.

In *Commentarii de Bello Gallico* Caesar reflects with great foresight that should the Germani "by degrees become accustomed to cross the Rhine, and that a great body of them should come into Gaul, it would be dangerous to the Roman people that wild and savage men would not be likely to restrain themselves, after they had possessed themselves of all Gaul, from going forth into the province and thence marching into Italy."

With this, Caesar sent a message to Ariovistus insisting on a summit conference in a neutral location. The German leader, styled as "king and friend" by the Roman Senate, snidely replied that "if he himself had need of anything from Caesar, he would have gone to him; and that if Caesar wanted anything from him he ought to come to him."

Caesar responded to the snub by reminding Ariovistus that he had been "treated with so much kindness" by the Roman people, and that if he were to repatriate the hostages he had taken from the Aedui and other Gallic tribes, the "Roman people will entertain a perpetual feeling of favor and friendship toward him." However, Caesar added that if Ariovistus didn't do as he asked, Caesar would act "consistently with the interests of the Republic [to] protect the Aedui and the other friends of the Roman people."

Ariovistus replied that "the right of war was that they who had conquered should govern those whom they had conquered, in what manner they pleased; that in that way the Roman people were wont to govern the nations which they had conquered, not according to the dictation of any other, but according to their own discretion.... Caesar was doing a great injustice, in that by his arrival he was making his [Ariovistus's] revenues less valuable to him."

Caesar must have been particularly perturbed that Ariovistus not only refused his demands but had the audacity to complain that Caesar was costing him tax revenue.

Caesar had even more reason to be infuriated when he learned that Ariovistus was preparing to march against the strategically important Gallic city of Vesontio, about 75 miles west of the Rhine, clearly planning to seize even more of Gaul.

Caesar mobilized his six legions for a forced march, planning to head Ariovistus off by reaching Vesontio first and establishing and provisioning a garrison to defend the city. As Caesar himself notes, troops in the Roman army had an ominous feeling about facing off against the Germani. Probably because of their potential foe's reputation for ruthlessness and brutality, some of the Roman legionaries expressed such reservations about a potential battle that Caesar had to take time for a reassuring pep talk. The Germani may have thrashed the Gauls, Caesar said, but they were no match for the Roman army.

A week later both armies were nearing the city, passing through the deep, dark forests of the Vosges Mountains. When they were about two dozen miles apart, Ariovistus sent a message to Caesar saying that now was a good time for the conference that Caesar had previously proposed.

Caesar agreed. He later acknowledged that he believed that Ariovistus "was now returning to a rational state of mind," and this was an opportunity to defuse the situation without a fight.

Ariovistus insisted that Caesar "should not bring any footsoldier with him to the conference," as he feared "being ensnared by him through treachery." This shows how much the formidable warlord actually dreaded the Roman army. He did agree that the two sides could be accompanied by cavalry, probably aware that Caesar was relying on Aeduan horsemen because Roman legions were an infantry force that depended upon auxiliary cavalry.

Caesar responded by mounting his favored Legio X foot soldiers on horseback. The legionaries joked that Caesar "did more for them than he had promised; he had promised to have Legio X in place of his praetorian cohort; but he now converted them into [cavalry]."

They met on a large "mound of earth," perhaps a neolithic mound, in an open field. Caesar opened by reminding Ariovistus that the Senate had designated him as a "friend and king" but added that the Aedui were long-standing friends of the Romans', and that it "was the custom of the Roman people to desire not only that its allies and friends should lose none of their property, but be advanced in influence, dignity, and honor."

As he had said in writing earlier, Caesar now insisted face to face that Ariovistus "should not make war either upon the Aedui or their allies, that he should restore the hostages; that if he could not send back to their country any part of the Germani, he should at all events suffer none of them any more to cross the Rhine."

Ariovistus shot back that "he had crossed the Rhine not of his own accord, but on being invited and sent for by the Gauls; that he had not left home and kindred without great expectations and great rewards; that he had settlements in Gaul, granted by the Gauls themselves; that the hostages had been given by their goodwill; that he took by right of war the tribute which conquerors are accustomed to impose on the conquered; that he had not made war upon the Gauls, but the Gauls upon him; that all the states of Gaul came to attack him."

He accused Caesar of "feigning friendship" with the Aedui to keep an army in Gaul, when his true purpose was to crush Ariovistus.

As the two men parried with words, their respective cavalry escorts were growing restless, so Caesar wrapped up the meeting. He sensed that a fight might break out. Although he assumed that his Legio X men would win such a battle, he feared that afterward it might be said that he had tricked Ariovistus to his death under the guise of agreeing to the conference.

Two days later, when a decisive battle had still not materialized, Caesar sent two of his young officers to Ariovistus's camp in an effort to arrange yet another summit conference. The men were Marcus Mettius, who apparently knew Ariovistus from earlier contacts, and Gaius Valerius Procillus, Caesar's translator and a second-generation Roman citizen who was ethnically Celtic. Instead of receiving them as diplomats, Ariovistus chained them up as spies and openly discussed how to kill them.

Caesar waited, allowing Ariovistus to make the next move, and the next after that. For five days the German moved his camp closer to that of the Romans, as Caesar watched and waited. Ariovistus launched probing movements against the Roman line with his cavalry that Caesar parried but to which he did not overreact. Ariovistus even camped a contingent of his force in a way that cut the Roman supply line.

Caesar organized his forces for battle. Placing four legions in two lines opposite the main German force, he pulled two legions back to fortify and guard a Roman camp that was untouched when Ariovistus cut the Roman supply line.

Meanwhile, the Germanic force was organized along tribal lines, with each tribe commanded and organized as a separate regiment, or the rough equivalent of the individual Roman legion. In addition to the Harudes, and Ariovistus's own Suebi people, the Germanic tribes present in the encampment included the Marcomanni, Nemetes, Sedusii, Triboci, and Vangiones.

As the Roman legionaries built and fortified their lines, and prepared for battle, Ariovistus sent his cavalry, supported by an equal number of light infantry (Caesar estimates a total of 16,000 men) to harass them. This involved minor skirmishing, as neither side was ready to launch the primary assault that would bring the decisive battle. While Ariovistus did launch a sizable attack against the smaller Roman reserve camp, he missed an opportunity to strike with his main force while the Romans were still getting ready for battle. As Caesar later learned, Ariovistus held back because his soothsayers told him to wait for the new moon, as it would bring good luck.

The next day Caesar was ready. He took the initiative, sending the four armed legions in his front line on a march toward the primary German encampment. He personally took command of the two legions on the Roman right wing.

Though it was not yet a new moon, Ariovistus realized that he must act, so he deployed his troops into a battle line, with each of the German tribes occupying its place in the phalanx. Caesar reports that the Germani flanked the troops with supply wagons on which were German women who, "with disheveled hair and in tears, entreated the soldiers, as they went forward to battle, not to deliver them into slavery to the Romans."

Caesar gave the signal and his legionaries went on the attack. Almost immediately, Ariovistus responded with a rushing counterattack. The battle was joined so quickly that the Roman javelin throwers didn't have a chance to throw against the lead elements of the German force. The throwers then drew their swords and waded into the German phalanx.

Vicious hand-to-hand combat ensued, in which Caesar reports, "Very many of our soldiers...leaped upon the phalanx, and with their hands tore away the shields, and wounded the enemy from above." Although the Germani were pushed back on the left, they forced the Romans back on the right.

The cavalry units, meanwhile, continued to skirmish around the periphery of the battlefield. The horsemen, who naturally had a better overview of the action, included a young officer named Publius Licinius Crassus, who was coincidentally the son of Caesar's fellow triumvir Marcus Licinius Crassus. The young Crassus could see where the Roman line was being threatened, and he acted. Though it was above his pay grade to do so, he took the initiative of ordering the two reserve legions into action.

Caesar credits the young officer's quick thinking with helping to turn the battle, writing in *Commentarii de Bello Gallico*, with almost audible relief, that "thereupon the engagement was renewed, and all the enemy turned their backs, nor did they cease to flee until they arrived at the river Rhine, about 50 miles from that place."

Indeed, rather than withdrawing to regroup, the Germani fell into a full-scale retreat across the river. Some, including Ariovistus, found boats to use in getting across, but many attempted to swim. Many, perhaps most, were killed by the Romans at the battle site. Of the civilians in the German camp, some got away, but others did not. Both of Ariovistus's wives, the German and the Gaul, were killed trying to escape, as was one of his daughters. The second daughter was taken captive.

The two Roman emissaries who had been taken prisoner by the Germani as spies were both recovered alive but still bound in chains. As Caesar wrote, finding Gaius Valerius Procillus alive afforded Caesar "no less pleasure than the victory itself," because Procillus was "a man of the first rank in the province of Gaul."

When the news of Caesar's triumph in the Battle of the Vosges, and of Ariovistus's retreat, spread east of the Rhine, German tribes that had been planning a move to Gaul canceled their travel plans. As for Ariovistus himself, he never again emerged as an important leader. He seems to have hidden out for a while in the Black Forest and is reported to have died within the ensuing four years. Publius Cornelius Tacitus, in his AD 98 book *De Origine et Situ Germanorum (The Origin and Situation of the Germans)* observes that German soldiers who retreated, leaving their shields on the battlefield, often committed suicide or were executed. "Traitors and deserters are hanged on trees," observes Tacitus. "The coward, the unwarlike, the man stained with abominable vices, is plunged into the mire of the morass."

Caesar put his legions into winter quarters near Vesontio and left his second in command, the legatus Titus Atius Labienus, in charge. Caesar then returned to spend the winter of 58–57 BC in Cisalpine Gaul, which he calls "Hither Gaul" in *Commentarii de Bello Gallico*, pondering the next move in his conquest of the rest of Gaul.

Julius Caesar had achieved much in his two Gallic campaigns of 58 BC. He had done more than simply beat a German warlord in a single major battle. The victory over Ariovistus was every bit the resounding reversal of German resettlement, just as Caesar's victory at Bibracte had been against Helvetii migration. He had curbed Germanic migration indefinitely.

In one season Caesar and his legions had changed the course of European history—or, depending upon one's perspective, he had *prevented* two major changes, these being the migration into present-day France by the ancestors of the modern Swiss and by the ancestors of the modern Germans.

As a practical matter, within all Gaul, Caesar's reputation as a military leader had become legend.

There would be more to come.

CHAPTER 7

Confronting the Belgae

STRATEGICALLY, JULIUS CAESAR UNDERSTOOD THAT IN 57 BC HE
had to achieve a comprehensive victory over the Gallic northern European tribes west of the Rhine in order to consolidate
his conquests of 58 BC. Doing so sooner rather than later he
would head off the possibility that the disparate tribes might
unite into a coalition, as the Germani had under Ariovistus and
the Suebi. Of specific concern for Caesar in 57 BC would be the
Belgae tribes. One of the three principal divisions of the Gallic
people, according to Caesar's reckoning, they occupied the region
roughly encompassed by modern Belgium and France's Picardy
and Normandy Regions.

As he writes in *Commentarii de Bello Gallico*, Caesar believed that
"the greater part of the Belgae were sprung from the Germani, and
that having crossed the Rhine at an early period, they had settled
there, on account of the fertility of the country, and had driven out
the Gauls who inhabited those regions." He added that the Belgae

"assumed to themselves great authority and haughtiness in military matters."

As had been the case with the Helvetii and Germani the previous year, the aggressiveness of his potential foes would provide Caesar with the pretext for offensive actions. Throughout the winter he received intelligence reports from Titus Atius Labienus at the Roman winter quarters north of Transalpine Gaul. Among these reports came warning that the Belgae might be arming to attack the Romans.

Caesar enlarged his command by two additional legions and prepared to resume operations in Gaul after the spring thaw; he made the march north from Cisalpine Gaul to the border of modern Belgium in about two weeks.

To accomplish the goal of engaging and defeating the Belgic tribes individually before they could form a unified force, Caesar adopted what was essentially a search-and-destroy strategy. He would march against certain specific fortified locations in the hope of drawing the tribes into battle as he marched. He banked on denying the advantage to the Belgae by making his legions a moving target. He would make his own army harder to hit, and he hoped to engage the various Gallic tribes individually and knock them off one by one.

As Caesar theorizes in *Commentarii de Bello Gallico,* the Belgae were "entering into a confederacy against the Roman people; first, because they feared that, after all Gaul was subdued, our army would be led against them; secondly, because they were instigated by several of the Gauls; some of whom as [on the one hand] they had been unwilling that the Germani should remain any longer in Gaul, so [on the other] they were dissatisfied that the army of the Roman people should pass the winter in it, and settle there."

As pleased as the Gauls were at the Romans having ousted the Helvetii and preventing the Germans from settling in their lands, they were definitely *displeased* by the prospect of having the Romans putting down roots there. Among the tribes of the Belgae, Caesar reckoned the Bellovaci to be the "most powerful among them in valor and influence," while he considered the Nervii to be "the most warlike."

Caesar learned as he rode north that the Remi were among the friendliest. Reckoned by Caesar to be the nearest of the Belgae to Gaul, the Remi had their capital at Durocortum, which is now Reims, France. They sent Iccius and Antebrogius, the "principal persons of the state, as their ambassadors" to Caesar, explaining that "they surrendered themselves and all their possessions to the protection and disposal of the Roman people."

They went on to insist that "they had neither combined with the rest of the Belgae, nor entered into any confederacy against the Roman people." They told Caesar that they were prepared to give hostages, obey his commands, receive him into their towns, and aid him "with corn and other things."

From the Remi. Caesar gained intelligence regarding the Belgae order of battle that proved quite comprehensive. He learned that the Bellovaci could muster 100,000 armed men, and they had promised 60,000 to the war effort in exchange for overall command of operations against the Romans. This indicated that the Belgae coalition that Caesar feared was starting to coalesce.

In addition, the Nervii and Suessiones had each committed 50,000 troops, while there would be 25,000 Morini, 19,000 Aduatuci, 9,000 Menapii, and 10,000 each from the Ambiani, Caleti, Velocasses, and Veromandui. These would be augmented by 40,000 troops from smaller tribes such as the Caeraesi, Condrusi, Eburones, and Paemani.

Against this amalgam of forces numbering nearly 300,000, Caesar's eight legions numbered about 40,000, plus his auxiliaries, which, he noted, included some Numidian and Cretan archers, as well as some Balearian slingers. The Romans could also count on support from the Aedui, the Roman allies commanded by Caesar's friend Divitiacus. Nevertheless, the Belgae outnumbered his force by as much as 6 to 1, a clear illustration of why Caesar hoped to be able to attack before a theoretical alliance could be molded into a coalition with a single unified command. With Divitiacus he discussed the necessity that "the forces of the enemy should be divided, so that it might not be necessary to engage with so large a number at one time."

As the first objective in his search-and-destroy strategy, Caesar picked the largest of the Belgae armies—the Bellovaci. As his own legions drew the Bellovaci army away from the defense of its homeland, Caesar sent the Aedui to "lay waste" to their territories.

However, as this strategy was being implemented, the Bellovaci moved eastward to attack the homes of the Remi, also Caesar's allies. As Caesar led his own forces northward across the Aisne River to search and destroy, the Bellovaci attacked the city of Iccius, the Remi chief, who sent a desperate message to the Romans to say that "unless assistance were sent to him he could not hold out any longer."

Caesar sent some archers and some slingers to relieve the siege, but this only compelled the Bellovaci to go elsewhere to attack and burn some smaller settlements of the Remi, who ran to the Roman camp for safety. As the Bellovaci and the Romans closed in on one another, they began probing one another's supply lines with cavalry. This resulted in some skirmishing, but the major battle that both sides expected would not occur for several days.

Caesar, meanwhile, had located a hill that he deemed "naturally convenient and suitable for marshaling an army," and on either side he "drew a cross trench of about four hundred paces, and at the extremities of that trench built forts." Aware that the Bellovaci had been lured close, he wanted to draw them into a fight in terrain that favored the Romans. As the two sides drew up on opposite sides of a swamp, he put his two newest legions into the fortified positions under the command of the legatus Quintus Titurius Sabinus.

When the Bellovaci attempted to outflank the Roman fortified positions by sending some troops across the Aisne River, Caesar himself led a Roman cavalry contingent to intercept them. Supported by Numidian archers, Caesar's horsemen struck the Bellovaci in the river, killing many. As other troops clambered over the bodies of the dead in an effort to get across the river, the mounted Romans surrounded them and, in Caesar's own words, cut them to pieces.

The remaining Bellovaci pulled out in a disorganized fashion and headed for home—they had failed to outflank Caesar, and they had learned that the Aedui were on the offensive against Belgic territory. As Caesar smirked, they departed "with great noise and confusion, in no fixed order, nor under any command, since each sought for himself the foremost place in the journey, and hastened to reach home, they made their departure appear very like a flight."

He then ordered Labienus, his second in command, to follow the Bellovaci closely with three legions and initiate a running attack against their rear guard. As Caesar recounts, "As soon as the noise was heard, [the Bellovaci] broke their ranks, and, to a man, [saved themselves by fleeing]. Thus without any risk [to themselves] our men killed as great a number of them as the length of the day allowed; and at sunset desisted from the pursuit."

Having decimated the Bellovaci, Caesar would march to, and take down, their capital city of Bratuspantium (now Beauvais, in France's Picardy region). On his way, however, the next target on Caesar's search and destroy checklist was the fortified capital city of the Suessiones, called Noviodunum (now Soissons). Parenthetically, this place was just one of several Gallic cities with this name which Caesar mentions, as "Noviodunum" literally means "hill fort."

On the day following his battle in the bloody waters of the Aisne, Caesar led his legions into the fertile fields of Suessiones country. Though lightly defended, Noviodunum was protected by high walls and a broad moat that Caesar decided could not be assaulted by infantry alone. Therefore he quickly put the legionaries to work constructing siege towers and making preparations for an attack. This apparently astounded the defenders. Caesar writes that, "amazed by the greatness of the works, such as they had neither seen nor heard of before, and struck also by the dispatch of the Romans," the Suessiones promptly surrendered, begging to be spared and offering up the sons of their king as hostages.

Caesar now moved on toward Bratuspantium. When the Romans were about five miles from the town, Caesar reports, "all the old men, going out of the town, began to stretch out their hands" in surrender. As the Romans began to set up camp outside the city walls, Caesar was greeted by the boys and the women, who streamed out, and "with outstretched hands, after their custom, begged peace from the Romans."

At this point Divitiacus of the Aedui went to Caesar to ask for clemency for the Bellovaci, explaining that in previous times the

Aedui and Bellovaci had been friends. Out of respect for Divitiacus, Caesar said that he would agree to this if all the warriors surrendered, and if he was given 600 hostages.

With the capitulation of the Bellovaci and the Suessiones, this left only the Nervii among the big three of the Belgae armies. They were next on Caesar's hit list.

Of the Nervii, Caesar wrote, "There was no access for merchants to them; that they suffered no wine and other things tending to luxury to be imported; because, they thought that by their use the mind is enervated and the courage impaired.... They were a savage people and of great bravery.... They upbraided and condemned the rest of the Belgae who had surrendered themselves to the Roman people and thrown aside their national courage." Furthermore, they "openly declared they would neither send ambassadors, nor accept any condition of peace."

Caesar turned north from Bratuspantium, marching east along a river known to the Romans as the Sabis, today known as the Selle. This put him on a direct line to the fields that would become the battlefields of the western front in World War I.

Within a few days Roman reconnaissance teams located the Nervii; they were preparing for battle in a forest on the northeast side of the Sabis, only about ten miles from the Roman camp. The army of the Nervii was supplemented by warriors from the neighboring Atrebates and Veromandui tribes, forming the sort of Belgic coalition of which Caesar was wary. Their total number, according to Caesar's probably exaggerated estimate, was 60,000 men. They had stashed their women and children in a nearby marsh, where they would be safe from a Roman attack. Caesar also notes that his own eight legions were now augmented by various contingents of Gallic, as well as Belgic, troops. These probably included Aedui as well as Remi.

The Romans set out for the Sabis, Caesar leading the way with his cavalry, accompanied by six legions. Two other legions followed behind with the supply train. When the vanguard was within sight of the river, the Romans prepared to set up camp on high ground sloping down toward the water.

At this point they were directly across from the woods where the Nervii and their allies were lying in wait, organized under the Nervii commander Boduognatus. According to Caesar, a few Belgic horsemen could be seen, but most of the enemy troops were infantry and heavily camouflaged, "having cut young trees, and bent them, by means of their numerous branches [extending] on to the sides, and the quickbriars and thorns springing up between them, had made these hedges present a fortification like a wall, through which it was not only impossible to enter, but even to penetrate with the eye."

The Nervii were on the left wing of the Belgic line, with the Atrebates on the right and the Veromandui in the middle.

Using the arrival of the supply wagons at the campsite as their signal, the Nervii launched their attack, dashing toward the Romans through the waist-deep waters of the Sabis. Even Caesar was surprised by the overpowering speed of the assault, writing in *Commentarii de Bello Gallico* that the Nervii "ran down to the river with such incredible speed that they seemed to be in the woods, the river, and close upon us almost at the same time. And with the same speed they hastened up the hill to our camp."

As Caesar acknowledged, the Roman cavalry screen closest to the river was "easily routed and thrown into confusion."

He goes on to explain that he "had every thing to do at one time: the standard to be displayed, which was the sign when it was necessary to run to arms; the signal to be given by the trumpet; the soldiers to be called off from the works; those who had proceeded some distance for the purpose of seeking materials for the rampart, to be summoned; the order of battle to be formed; the soldiers to be encouraged; the watchword to be given."

The surprise attack had caught the Romans thoroughly off guard, and the Nervii knew it. This certainly contributed both to their enthusiasm and their confidence. The Romans were not in battle order, and most had shed their helmets and gear. The enemy quickly surrounded the scattered Roman troops and hammered them hard.

Had it not been for their exceptional training, the Roman legions probably would have been quickly defeated. However, individual groups quickly set up defensive perimeters and fought back.

"Such was the shortness of the time," Caesar writes, recalling how unprepared his men were for battle, "and so determined was the mind of the enemy on fighting, that time was wanting not only for affixing the military insignia, but even for putting on the helmets and drawing off the covers from the shields. To whatever part any one by chance came from the works, and whatever standards he saw first, at these he stood, lest in seeking his own company he should lose the time for fighting."

As the Nervii attacked, with Boduognatus himself leading, they struck the positions of Legio VII and Legio XII on the Roman right. The Romans found themselves pushed, then outflanked. The situation was nearly catastrophic. As Caesar later noted, all the centurions in IV Cohort of Legio XII were killed in action, and nearly all the centurions in the other cohorts either died or were wounded.

The Nervii reached the encampment in the Roman rear and were in possession of the Roman supply train. Though the Roman legionaries held fast, the Numidian and other allied auxiliaries panicked and retreated. The outcome was in doubt.

Caesar, who was in the thick of the action on the Roman right, near the hard-pressed Legio VII, acted to link that legion into a square with Legio XII and others, so as to provide a solid, four-sided defensive block.

It was a time of terror and of bravery. In his recollections of the battle in *Commentarii de Bello Gallico,* and probably in a dispatch issued at the time, Caesar singled out Publius Sextius Baculus, a centurion in Legio XII, calling him "a very valiant man, who was so exhausted by many and severe wounds, that he was already unable to support himself."

Despite his injuries, Baculus

perceived that the rest were slackening their efforts, and that some, deserted by those in the rear, were retiring from the battle and avoiding the weapons; that the enemy though advancing from the lower ground, were not relaxing in front, and were pressing hard on both flanks; he also perceived that the affair was at a crisis, and that there was not any reserve which could be brought up, having therefore snatched a shield from one of the soldiers in the rear, for he himself had come without a shield, he advanced to the front of the line, and addressing the centurions by name, and encouraging the rest of the soldiers, he ordered them to carry forward the standards, and extend the companies, that they might the more easily use their swords. On his arrival, as hope was brought to the soldiers and their courage restored, while every one for his own part, in the sight of his general, desired to exert his utmost energy, the impetuosity of the enemy was a little checked.

As terrible as things were in the collapse of the Roman right, elsewhere the opposite prevailed. Though the Nervii attack had been swift, ferocious, and successful, similar attacks by the Veromandui and Atrebates had stalled almost immediately. Acting quickly, the legionaries of Legio IX and Legio X, who were on the Roman far left, not only stopped the Atrebates cold but quickly launched their own cross-river assault in the opposite direction. Meanwhile, Legio VIII and Legio XI routed the Veromandui in the center.

The whole battlefield had rotated clockwise by 45 degrees. As Boduognatus led the Nervii south across the river on the southeastern edge of the battlefield, Romans under Labienus crossed northward at the northwestern end of the battlefield. As Boduognatus came around the Roman right flank clockwise to plunge into the Roman camp, Labienus came clockwise around the right flank of the Atrebates to plunge deep into the Belgic coalition camp.

When Labienus reached the high ground and captured the Belgic camp, he looked back to see what was happening in the Roman rear and promptly sent Legio X back across to aid Caesar.

The arrival of these reinforcements provided an immense boost for the morale of the Romans on the southwest side. Caesar, who witnessed the scene, wrote that "so great a change of matters was made, that our men, even those who had fallen down exhausted with wounds, leaned on their shields, and renewed the fight: then the camp retainers, though unarmed, seeing the enemy completely dismayed, attacked."

Caesar added that the auxiliary cavalrymen, who had panicked earlier, also reentered the fight so "that they might by their valor blot the disgrace of their flight, thrust themselves before the legionary soldiers in all parts of the battle."

As the reserve legions arrived from the southwest and entered the fray where the Nervii had circled into the Roman rear, the Romans at last gained the advantage.

The Nervii, now surrounded themselves, fought bravely and defiantly, even using the bodies of their dead as breastworks.

Finally, it was over, with the Nervii, in Caesar's words, "being almost reduced to annihilation."

Caesar's fortune in the Battle of the Sabis River was clearly a victory snatched from the jaws of defeat. The snatching was the sum of several factors. It was part luck, of course, and a large measure of bravery, exemplified by such men as Publius Sextius Baculus. The other factor was the cool battlefield leadership of Labienus and of Caesar himself.

Mainly, however, this victory, in the wake of a demoralizing surprise attack, came down to the legionaries themselves, and to Roman professional army doctrine. In Gallic combat experience, to catch an enemy while he had laid down his arms to make camp was a prescription for achieving a total rout. Attacked with such sudden swiftness, any other army of that era would have been reduced to the chaos of every man for himself. But not the Romans. This was a point at which the generations of discipline and Roman training doctrine truly shone.

Unit cohesion had been drummed into the legionaries, and it had stuck with them. As a result they did not desert one another that afternoon on the Sabis. Each centuria and each cohort was a self-contained entity that responded as one man.

As was Caesar's practice, each centurion was under standing orders not to step away from his unit until that unit's fortifications were ready. This meant that each commander was with his men. Just as each legionary knew what to do, so too did each commander. None was dependent on Caesar for orders. There was no looking around for a signal from higher authority.

What surprised the Nervii on the Sabis was unusual in the first century BC, but in recent centuries this balance of unit cohesion and individual initiative has been a characteristic of the best organized, best trained, and best disciplined of the world's military forces. All soldiers know their roles so that they can function as part of the overall structure of a command, but at the same time each soldier and each commander at the platoon, company, and regimental levels can think strategically, and both act and lead without having to wait for direction from a higher level.

Competent leadership at the top and bravery beyond the call of duty are important, but the fabric of the army itself carried the day on the Sabis.

CHAPTER 8

Unfinished Business

ONE BY ONE THEY FELL. JULIUS CAESAR'S STRATEGY OF MOVING continuously, hitting the major Belgic tribes in the field before they could form a unified force, had worked. By taking down the largest of the Belgic armies first, he had progressively reduced the probability that the Belgae would form themselves into an effective foe.

Caesar had initially defeated the Bellovaci and the Suessiones, which were, by his own prewar reckoning, two of the three largest Belgic armies. Then the Nervii, also among the big three, had managed to join with the smaller Veromandui and the Atrebates tribes before Caesar met them. Together they had come closer to beating the Romans than had the others, but when the Battle of the Sabis River was over, Caesar had prevailed. He had now defeated roughly half the armed strength that the Belgic tribes possessed at the beginning of the 57 BC campaigning season, but he was not yet finished.

Had the Nervii waited, they might have also been joined by the Aduatuci, who were en route to join them when the Sabis River fight took place. Whether they might have tipped the balance on the Sabis will never be known. Neither is how close they were to the Sabis, but it seems they were just a matter of days from linking up with their allies. When news of the Nervii defeat reached the Aduatuci, they halted their advance, abandoned their villages, and withdrew their army to a fortified hilltop citadel overlooking the Meuse River in what is now the Belgian city of Namur. Caesar's prewar estimate of their strength stood at 19,000 armed men.

In *Commentarii de Bello Gallico* Caesar describes the Aduatuci citadel as "eminently fortified by nature. While this town had on all sides around it very high rocks and precipices, there was left on one side a gently ascending approach, of not more than 200 feet in width; which place they had fortified with a very lofty double wall: besides, they had placed stones of great weight and sharpened stakes upon the walls."

After some initial skirmishing outside the fortified walls, the Romans began work on a siege tower in preparation for a major assault. As Caesar recalls, the Aduatuci reaction to the tower was one of amusement, not trepidation.

"For what purpose was so vast a machine constructed at so great a distance?" Caesar recalls the Aduatuci taunting. "With what hands...with what strength did they, especially [as they were] men of such very small stature...place against [our] walls a tower of such great weight?"

However, their derisive tone changed when they saw the Romans efficiently moving the siege tower toward the city. Says Caesar, whose turn it now was for a laugh, "They did not believe the Romans waged war without divine aid, since they were able to move forward machines of such a height with so great speed, and thus fight from close quarters....They resigned themselves and all their possessions to [our] disposal; that they begged and earnestly entreated one thing, that if perchance, agreeable to [our] clemency and humanity, which they had heard of from others, [we] should resolve that the Aduatuci were to be spared."

Caesar replied to their proposal that if they were going to surrender, they would have to do it before the first Roman battering ram touched their walls. He added that there was no condition of surrender, "except upon their arms being delivered up." He told them that he would give them the same deal he had given the Nervii, that he would "command their neighbors not to offer any injury to those who had surrendered to the Roman people."

The Aduatuci responded by dumping a large stock of weaponry into a trench outside their walls and stacking an equal part on their rampart walls. As Caesar writes, the Aduatuci "enjoyed peace for that day." What he did not know as he accepted their surrender was that they had secretly hidden a sizable number of weapons.

In the middle of the night the Aduatuci attacked the Romans camped outside the city walls, hoping to catch them off guard. In the fighting that ensued, Caesar estimates that the Romans killed 4,000 Aduatuci before forcing them back inside the city walls. The following day the Romans captured the walled city for the second time. This time the goodwill that Caesar had been predisposed to offer the Aduatuci a day earlier no longer prevailed. According to him, the Romans captured 53,000 Aduatuci, 70 percent of them civilians. They were all sold into slavery, with the proceeds helping to fund future Roman campaigns. Selling captured soldiers and civilians into slavery was common practice in the ancient world. The Romans did it, as had the Greeks and Macedonians before them. That Caesar chose *not* to do so on several occasions throughout his later conquests was considered both magnanimous and unusual.

With the defeat of the Bellovaci, Suessiones, and Nervii, and now with the elimination of the Aduatuci, Belgic resistance dissipated. It appeared there was nothing left but to celebrate, but appearances were deceiving.

In Rome, Caesar's second year of victories in Gaul had made him a popular hero of the highest order. The Senate was beside itself with praise, heaping honors upon the man who was, in 57 BC, the republic's favorite conquering hero. Caesar bragged proudly, and without modesty, that "a Supplicatio [Thanksgiving] of fifteen days was decreed for those achievements... [an honor] which before that time had been conferred on none."

He was now eager to get back to Italy to relish his Supplicatio. Indeed, he was so keen that when German tribes whom he had not even fought came across the Rhine to lay themselves at his mercy, and offer him tribute, he told them to come back later. As he writes in *Commentarii de Bello Gallico*: "These things being achieved, [and] all Gaul being subdued, so high an opinion of this war was spread among the barbarians, that ambassadors were sent to Caesar by those nations who dwelt beyond the Rhine, to promise that they would give hostages and execute his commands."

Winter was coming on, and Caesar was eager to be feted under warm Mediterranean skies. He headed south, leaving his lieutenants in charge of tying up loose ends and settling the legions into winter quarters.

One of the loose ends that seemed easily dealt with was the northwestern corner of Gaul in Armorica (now the area comprised mainly of France's Brittany Peninsula). Even before he went after the Aduatuci, Caesar had sent the young officer Publius Crassus (the son of his old ally Marcus Licinius Crassus) with Legio VII to subdue the Gauls of Armorica. Specifically, Crassus was tasked with operations against tribes that included the Veneti in Brittany and the Unelli (also called Venelli) of the nearby Cotentin Peninsula. Historians viewing the campaign with 20–20 hindsight wonder about Caesar's decision to send such a small force into so large a region, not to mention that Legio VII was an odd choice, as it had borne the brunt of the Nervii beating at the Sabis River.

Another loose end that seemed easily handled in the fall of 57 BC was Caesar's desire to secure a particular trade route through the Alps. As Caesar himself recalled, it was a road on which Roman merchants "had been accustomed to travel with great danger, and under great imposts." He sent Legio XII under the legatus Servius Sulpicius Galba to make this road safe for commercial traffic, and to pacify the area roughly between the crest of the Alps, where the Helvetii lived, and the land of the Allobroges people in the Rhone River valley. To accomplish his mission Galba would have to subdue the Gallic tribes who lived east of Lacus Lemannus (Lake Geneva), including the Nantuatae.

As Caesar writes in a terse summary, Galba "fought some successful battles and stormed several of their forts, upon ambassadors being sent to him from all parts and hostages given and a peace concluded, [he was] determined to station two cohorts among the Nantuatae."

Galba decided that he would spend the winter in the mountains himself, setting up camp with the two cohorts in the crossroads village of Octodurus (now the Swiss city of Martigny), which Caesar described as "situated in a valley, with a small plain annexed to it,... bounded on all sides by very high mountains." Today the city is an important intersection of rail lines and highways connecting Switzerland, Italy, and France. Because the village was bisected by the Rhone River, Galba moved all the Nantuatae to one side, while he commandeered and fortified the other bank for his legionaries. Up to this point it all seemed fairly routine. It might have remained that way had Galba not insisted on taking children of the Nantuatae as hostages after the people had surrendered.

Several days later the Romans woke up to find that their Gallic neighbors had abandoned their part of Octodurus during the night. In the mountains above, the Romans observed an exceptionally huge contingent of Gallic warriors. Perhaps using eyewitness accounts, Caesar estimates—or, more likely, exaggerates—that the enemy force numbered 30,000. With only two cohorts, Galba's fighting strength would have been about 1,000 men.

Galba was in a dangerous predicament. His fortifications were not finished, nor were his winter quarters. He had only the two cohorts with which to face an enemy that had him surrounded, and he did not have sufficient provisions even for that small number. When he discussed the matter with his officers, some wanted to make a break for it by fighting their way out. The majority, however, felt that this should be saved for a last resort, and that they should stay put and fight a defensive action.

The enemy made the choice for them, attacking out of the mountains from all directions, while archers and rock throwers on the cliffs showered the Romans with projectiles. As Caesar later commented, "Our men at first, while their strength was fresh, resisted bravely." Wave after wave of the enemy surged against the Romans, inflicting serious damage but failing to overwhelm the Roman defenses. Caesar claims that his troops killed 10,000 Gallic warriors but makes no mention of Roman losses.

Finally, after six hours of nonstop fighting, the centurion Publius Sextius Baculus, whose bravery in the battle against Nervii had been singled out in Caesar's account, went to Galba and told him that it was time to try to flee this valley of death.

The escape succeeded. We know this because Galba survived, but we don't know the details. Caesar claims that the enemy who opposed the Romans were "put to flight...when panic stricken." It seems improbable that the remnants of a battered pair of cohorts could have done that to an army of 20,000, assuming Caesar's inflated numbers are accurate. In any case, as he got away, Galba abandoned Octodurus, a defeat in itself, to winter his Legio XII among the Allobroges in Transalpine Gaul.

Across Gaul in Armorica (Brittany), Publius Crassus was also going into winter quarters with his Legio VII, having failed to pacify the peninsula, just as Galba had failed to secure the future canton of Valais. Caesar's loose ends had not been tied off.

As Caesar was returning to Italy for his Supplicatio, he was justifiably congratulated for his great success against the Belgic armies. He had already been thinking ahead to a campaign in Illyricum in 56 BC, but this would not be possible. The loose ends that he had delegated to subordinates at the end of 57 BC had already become the unfinished business that would define his campaigning season in the coming year.

This would take him back to Gaul in 56 BC and would in turn evolve into campaigns in 55 BC that would set the course of European history for two millennia.

CHAPTER 9

The Veneti, the Aquitani, and the Corners of Gaul

WHEN JULIUS CAESAR HAD LEFT FOR ITALY IN THE FALL OF 57 BC, HE assumed that his mission in the northern part of Gaul had been accomplished. As he writes in *Commentarii de Bello Gallico,* he had "every reason to suppose that Gaul was reduced to a state of tranquility, the Belgae being overcome, the Germani expelled."

However, the "tranquility" of which Caesar writes so casually had *not* been achieved. The Gallic tribes that he had defeated personally may have remained pacified, but others, which he had considered peripheral, and of significantly lesser consequence, would prove in 56 BC to be anything but. When he thought that operations against these tribes were to be mere mopping up actions that could easily be relegated to subordinates, he was seriously mistaken.

Caesar's first challenge to Gallic tranquility in 56 BC was on the rough coast of Armorica (now Brittany). At the end of the previous year's campaigning season, when he had dispatched Publius Crassus with Legio VII to bring the tribes of Gaul's remote northwestern corner into line as Roman subjects, Caesar had assumed it to be a perfunctory operation. It had not been. Crassus had made some headway against some tribes, notably the Unelli, who occupied the Cotentin Peninsula, but had failed in his campaign to subdue the Veneti who dominated Armorica. As Caesar later came to understand, the Veneti were the key to Armorica. Their influence was, in his words, "by far the most considerable of any of the countries on the whole sea coast."

The Veneti lived on the south coast of the Armorica peninsula adjacent to the bay now called Morbihan. Their principal city, called Darioritum by the Romans, was in an area characterized by an extremely rugged coastline that is relentlessly lashed by Atlantic storms. For this reason navigating without smashing on the rocks is difficult for those not used to the nuances of the sea and coastline. The Veneti were, and the Romans were not.

Caesar himself provides an excellent overview of the maritime nature of the Veneti when he writes in *Commentarii de Bello Gallico* that they "have a very great number of ships, with which they have been accustomed to sail to Britannia, and [thus] excel the rest in their knowledge and experience of nautical affairs."

To defend themselves the Veneti occupied fortified outposts located on rocky promontories that were difficult to approach from land or sea. It is axiomatic in military science that terrain favors the defender, but the shoreline of the Veneti homeland was not simply a classic example of this maxim. It was an extreme example.

The Veneti also used these well-defended enclaves to control maritime traffic in the region. As Caesar notes,

Only a few ports lie scattered along that stormy and open sea, of which they are in possession, they [are able to control the maritime activities of any other tribe] who are accustomed to traffic in that sea.... The sites of their towns were generally such that, being placed on extreme points [of land] and on promontories, they neither had an approach by land when the tide had rushed in from the main ocean, which always happens twice in the space of twelve hours; nor by ships, because, upon the tide ebbing again, the ships were likely to be dashed upon the shoals.

In this, written in retrospect, Caesar expresses a comprehensive appreciation of the Veneti mastery of the tactical situation in the Armorica area that he almost certainly did not grasp when he sent Crassus to deal with them.

He adds, also after the fact, that the land approaches to the cities of the Veneti were as problematic as those by sea, and that the Romans went into Armorica without a full appreciation of the reality of the terrain. Caesar acknowledges that "the passes by land were cut off by estuaries, that the approach by sea was most difficult, by reason of our ignorance of the localities, [and] the small number of the harbors, and [the Veneti] trusted that our army would not be able to stay very long among them, on account of the insufficiency of corn."

In underestimating the Veneti and their allies, as well as the defense-friendly topography of their peninsula, Caesar and Crassus would have good company. In August 1944, seven weeks after the epic Allied invasion of nearby Normandy in World War II, General George Patton's US Third Army was tasked with capturing Brittany (Armorica) from the Germans as part of Allied Operation Cobra. Despite initial optimism, the Americans found to their dismay that things did not go as well or as quickly as they expected. Both Patton and Caesar misjudged the extent to which Brittany is an easily defensible battlefield, and each would spend much more time than anticipated in his campaign there.

The difficulties had begun when the Allied forces attempted to break out of the nearby Normandy beachheads, where they had seriously underestimated the terrain, in June and July 1944. The hedgerows of Normandy, which had looked on aerial photographs to be benign garden hedges, turned out to be tangled, almost impenetrable, walls of vegetation, often more than ten feet tall, that stopped tanks and troops alike. The hedgerows had yet to be planted in Caesar's time, but the situation in 1944 is illustrative of the types of problems that beset invading forces, including Caesar's, when they fail to reconnoiter the terrain where they will be operating.

As the Allies would two millennia later, Caesar found out the hard way that, in his words, "so much labor was spent in vain and that the flight of the enemy could not be prevented on the capture of their towns, and that injury could not be done them."

Key tactical objectives of the 1944 Brittany campaign were the major seaports, including those at Brest, Saint-Nazaire, and Lorient, that had been used by the German navy as important submarine bases throughout the war. Saint-Nazaire and Lorient flank Morbihan Bay, and as fortress cities they were the analog of the Veneti's fortified enclaves of 56 BC.

Patton's troops required a full week to reach Brest in August 1944, and another six weeks of terrible fighting and destruction to force the Germans to surrender there. As for Saint-Nazaire and Lorient on the Veneti coast, they were so well defended that the US Army gave up and acknowledged its failure to achieve its strategic objectives. Though they were surrounded and could no longer support offensive submarine operations, or contribute to the war effort, these German garrisons in Veneti country held out and did not surrender until May 9, 1945, one day after VE Day and the surrender of Nazi Germany.

Although the Allies had just conducted the biggest amphibious operation in history a hundred miles to the east, they wrote off a seaborne landing on the rugged coast of Brittany as potentially too costly. Because the Allies had attained mastery of the sea and had neutralized German maritime power in the area, they could afford to simply bypass the enemy forts at Saint-Nazaire and Lorient. Caesar could not afford to do this. In 56 BC the Veneti controlled the sea, so in order to further his strategic goals, Caesar would have to gain control of the water.

With this in mind Caesar had instructed Crassus to spend the winter building a navy, the first Roman fleet to conduct military operations outside the Mediterranean. The ships for this navy were built on the Loire River, which flows into the Atlantic at the base of the Armorica peninsula. The shipwrights, as well as the sailors for the flotilla, were recruited locally from tribes such as the Pictones and the Santones, who had previously submitted to Roman rule, and who were familiar with sailing the rugged coastline. Each ship would also carry a contingent of Roman soldiers who would function as boarding parties.

Caesar describes the Veneti ships as "built wholly of oak, and designed to endure any force and violence" rendered by the conditions in the Atlantic, and notes that the Romans designed their ships as if they were still in the Mediterranean. He states that the Roman fleet "excelled in speed alone, and the plying of the oars," acknowledging that in other respects the Veneti vessels "were more suitable and better adapted" to the coastal conditions. Another important difference was that while the Veneti ships depended on sails for propulsion, the Roman galleys were rowed by ranks of oarsmen.

Caesar's battle plan for his 56 BC Armorica campaign involved both land and sea components. Caesar himself would lead the land forces against the Veneti homeland, while the legatus Decimus Junius Brutus Albinus (not to be confused with Caesar's later archnemesis, Marcus Brutus) would be in command of the Roman fleet.

Caesar marched into the peninsula from the south, advancing to what is now Point St. Jacques on the south side of the Gulf of Morbihan, opposite the Veneti city of Darioritum. Brutus sailed northward from the mouth of the Loire.

The fleet of the Veneti, meanwhile, headed out of the Gulf of Morbihan and into Quiberon Bay, which separates the gulf from the Atlantic. There the two navies met in battle within sight of Caesar on the shore. He notes that the Veneti had 220 ships but does not mention Roman numbers. Subsequent estimates have guessed that the Romans were outnumbered by about 2 to 1.

The Romans discovered that the Veneti ships were higher than the Romans', making it easier for the Veneti to hurl projectiles from above as the vessels closed on one another. However, the Veneti were caught off guard when the Romans began attacking with, as Caesar describes in detail, "sharp hooks inserted into and fastened upon poles, of a form not unlike the hooks used in attacking town walls."

These were cast into the rigging on the Veneti ships. Once hooked, the masts and yardarms could be pulled down, leaving the vessels essentially dead in the water and at the mercy of waves, tides, and Roman rowers. Though there were two or more Veneti ships to each Roman ship in the closely packed melee, the Romans still had the ability to maneuver. Roman troops swarmed over the Veneti ships, subduing their crews one by one.

By sunset the Veneti fleet had been defeated and destroyed. That day they had lost not just a battle but the war. The Roman victory was swift and complete, because the Veneti had bet everything on one battle. As Caesar observes, "They had collected in that one place whatever naval forces they had anywhere; and when these were lost, the survivors had no place to retreat to, nor means of defending their towns. They accordingly surrendered themselves and all their possessions."

Quiberon Bay was also the site of one of Britain's most decisive naval victories over the French, the turning point in the Seven Years War, on November 20, 1759. Like the Veneti, the French lost most of their fleet. By winning, the British headed off French plans to invade Britain. The outcome of the later battle was similar strategically to Caesar's naval victory, for it affected the balance of power in the region. The Veneti had dominated the maritime activities of the area, and hence its commerce, for as long as anyone could remember. Caesar's victory permanently sank them as a regional superpower, thereby altering the course of history in this corner of Europe. In 1759 the British victory confirmed British naval dominance and protected Britain from an invasion that would have changed history by tipping the balance in the long-running Anglo-French feud.

Caesar was ruthless against the now helpless Veneti people. Acting without his usual magnanimity, he massacred their leaders and "sold the rest for slaves." This harsh treatment was in part retribution for the difficult fight the Veneti had handed Caesar and partly a message to other tribes in the region that the Romans were not to be trifled with.

At the close of the Veneti campaign Caesar went back to the strategy that had served him well the year before against the Belgae: to go on the offensive against individual power centers, attempting to force decisive battles before those centers could be reinforced through the forming of battlefield coalitions. However, there was a key difference. In 57 BC he had campaigned in a relatively small region with his entire army. In 56 BC he chose to dispatch components of his total command to four widely separated corners of Gaul. These operations ranged from the proactive to reactive, from aggressive offensive actions to reactions intended to thwart moves made by the opposition.

Even before he had completely subdued the Veneti, Caesar sent Publius Crassus from Armorica due south to Aquitania on an offensive mission with cavalry and a dozen cohorts (the equivalent of one reinforced legion) of infantry.

Quintus Titurius Sabinus, leading three legions, marched into Normandy, where tribes previously quelled by Crassus had chosen Caesar's difficulty against the Veneti as an opportunity to rebel against the Romans.

Titus Atius Labienus, Caesar's second in command, took two legions to the Moselle River valley immediately west of the Rhine to deter Germani incursions in support of any potential Belgic revolt against Roman rule.

Caesar himself would return to the coastal northeast corner of Belgica to quell disturbances along the border with Germania.

Crassus's Aquitania operations were of particular interest to Caesar because, as I noted at the beginning of chapter 5, the area was one of the three parts of the Gaul that were unconquered when he started his conquests two years before. As he wrote on the opening page of *Commentarii de Bello Gallico,* Caesar considered those three parts of unconquered northern and central Gaul to be comprised of Belgica, Aquitania, and everything else. Geographically, Aquitania occupied the southwest corner of what is now France and corresponds roughly to France's Aquitaine Region. On Roman maps it was the land between Transalpine Gaul and the Atlantic Ocean, and north of the northern portion of the Iberian Peninsula that had not yet been incorporated into Roman Hispania.

Caesar had spent the entire campaigning season in 57 BC subduing Belgica. One might deduce from this that the 56 BC Aquitania operations were of equivalent importance, in Caesar's mind, to the 57 BC Belgica operations. He must have had a high opinion of the 25-year-old Crassus—or a low opinion of the Aquitani—because Caesar had used eight legions in Belgica, but he sent fewer than two against Aquitania. It is open to conjecture as to why Caesar picked Crassus for this command after the young man's earlier failure to subdue the Veneti. It may have been that he was the son of Marcus Crassus, Caesar's fellow triumvir, but the confidence he placed in him by giving him the Aquitaniaim job was probably derived less from this relationship than from the tactical and leadership skills that he exhibited during the earlier Gallic campaigns.

Ancient historians provide no clear idea of the relative numerical strength of the Aquitani compared with that of the Belgic tribes, so we must assume that the Aquitani were fewer and that Caesar had this information. It is also a safe assumption that the Aquitani did outnumber the small Roman force which Crassus had under his command. Perhaps flashing a wry smile, Caesar notes that Crassus's men desired that it "might be seen what they could accomplish without their general [Caesar] and without the other legions."

As the Bellovaci and Nervii had proved to be the key Roman adversaries among the Belgae, the principal tribe among the Aquitani were the Sotiates, who lived in the area south of the modern French city of Bordeaux. As Caesar describes them, the Sotiates, "relying on their former victories, imagined that the safety of the whole of Aquitania rested on their valor."

As Crassus marched into Aquitania, he would have been aware of the defeat and death of the proconsul Lucius Valerius Praeconinus, who had led a Roman army north from Transalpine Gaul on a similar expedition into the area five years earlier, an event that Caesar himself mentions in connection with the 56 BC operation.

The opening encounter between Crassus and the Sotiates involved a large-scale cavalry battle in which the Sotiates were overpowered. However, as the Roman cavalry pursued the retreating enemy into a narrow valley, the horsemen found themselves drawn into an infantry ambush. The Sotiate commander, Adcantuannus, had either prepared the battlefield for the contingency of a rout of his horsemen or deliberately planned for his men to break off the fight and lure the Romans into a trap.

Adcantuannus nonetheless lost the battle and was forced to withdraw into a fortified stronghold. Crassus responded by erecting siege towers and the two sides sparred for a while. The Sotiates even went so far as to tunnel beneath the siege towers in an attempt to collapse them.

Eventually, the Sotiates sent emissaries to the Romans offering to surrender. Crassus accepted and ordered them to begin stacking their arms. However, as this was being done, Adcantuannus and 600 men from his elite guard attacked the Romans. After a ferocious hand-to-hand battle, the Sotiate warlord capitulated and begged for mercy.

When news of the Sotiate defeat spread, other Aquitani tribes farther south began efforts to form a coalition to fight the Romans. As Caesar points out, many tribal military leaders in the area, especially the Cantabri from the Iberian Peninsula who fought with the Aquitani, had learned Roman tactics from the proconsul of Hispania two decades earlier.

Caesar also credits Crassus with making the right decision in keeping his relatively small force together while paying particular attention to maintaining his supply lines. In retrospect Caesar sees logistics as the key to the campaign, writing that "if the Romans, on account of the want of corn, should begin to retreat, [the Aquitani] intended to attack them while encumbered in their march and depressed in spirit," adding that the enemy "considered it safer to gain the victory without any wound, by besetting the passes [and] cutting off the provisions."

Crassus was careful to deny them such an opportunity. As the legionaries, marching southward into Aquitania, reached the limits of their logistical train, Crassus arranged his forces so as to draw the enemy into a fight. As Caesar writes, "Having drawn out all his forces at the break of day, and marshaled them in a double line, he posted the auxiliaries in the center, and waited to see what measures the enemy would take."

Caesar meanwhile credits the Aquitani with overconfidence, writing that "on account of their great number and their ancient renown in war, and the small number of our men, they supposed they might safely fight." He estimates their numbers at 50,000, which would have meant that Crassus was outnumbered by about 50 to 1. While Crassus may well have been outnumbered, this ratio seems improbable.

As part of his defensive plans, Crassus heavily fortified a section of the battlefield to give the appearance of being the primary Roman position. In fact, it was bait in a trap. Crassus had surrounded this section with troops hidden at a distance. As the battle ensued, the Aquitani finally overwhelmed the defenses at the bait site and poured into the center of the battlefield, only to find themselves surrounded by Roman troops. Crassus had meanwhile sent his cavalry around the outside of the battlefield to attack the lightly defended Aquitani camp.

The Roman victory was complete, with three-quarters of the Aquitani and Cantabri force either killed or captured. Crassus's cavalry managed also to pick off some of the retreating enemy before breaking off the pursuit at nightfall.

As Caesar summarizes, "Having heard of this battle, the greatest part of Aquitania surrendered itself to Crassus, and of its own accord sent hostages."

Meanwhile, in the north, Quintus Titurius Sabinus was marching into the hinterlands of what is now Normandy with a force nearly three times the size of that of Crassus. There the principal foe was the Unelli, who had surrendered to Publius Crassus prior to his earlier, ill-fated Veneti campaign, but who were now in revolt. The field of conflict was the Cotentin Peninsula, east of Brittany. In World War II the Cotentin would also be an important battleground, because it was immediately adjacent to the beaches where the Allied armies came ashore in Normandy on D-Day, June 6, 1944. The port of Cherbourg, located at the tip of the peninsula, became a key objective. For both Caesar and the Allies in World War II, subduing the peninsula was a part of the overall strategy of denying territory to the enemy. The Allies got an added bonus. Cherbourg, captured by American troops three weeks after the invasion, served as an important Allied supply port. Caesar's supply lines stretched over land in the opposite direction, so he did not need a port.

In the summer of 56 BC the Unelli army was commanded by a charismatic warlord named Viridovix, who had "collected a large and powerful army," including warriors from other nearby tribes. Caesar goes on to suggest that Viridovix became a magnet for individuals and factions from throughout the area who wanted to band together to fight the Romans. Caesar writes that the Aulerci and the Sexovii people, "having slain their senate because they would not consent to be promoters of the war, shut their gates [against the Romans] and united themselves to Viridovix; a great multitude besides of desperate men and robbers assembled out of Gaul from all quarters, whom the hope of plundering and the love of fighting had called away from husbandry and their daily labor."

As the Unelli and their allies arrayed against him, Sabinus kept to his camp, not launching a major action despite cavalry skirmishing on the perimeter. Because Sabinus refused to act, the enemy became ever bolder, and even within the Roman camp legionaries were starting to accuse their commander of spinelessness. However, this illusion of cowardice was intentionally and carefully crafted by Sabinus as part of a plan to seduce Viridovix into battle.

To cap his deception Sabinus chose a man from the ranks of his auxiliaries whom Caesar describes as "a certain suitable and crafty Gaul" to go over to Viridovix and pretend to be a deserter. The crafty Gaul painted a picture of apprehension and indecision in the Roman command tent. As Viridovix and his war council guffawed at the perceived weakness of the Roman officers, the crafty Gaul went on to share an actionable bit of intelligence. He whispered that Sabinus was planning to pull out the following night and retreat to Caesar's camp.

Viridovix gullibly accepted this story because, as Caesar points out, "men willingly believe what they wish."

In turn, the Unelli and their allies rejoiced "as if victory were fully certain," and prepared to attack the Roman camp, hurrying to do so before the Romans got away.

Within the Roman camp the legionaries were ready. Only a mile separated the respective camps, but Sabinus had situated his at the top of a slope, so that when the Unelli and their allies launched a ferocious running charge, they reached the Roman bulwark out of breath.

Sabinus then sprang his trap, flanking the panting, breathless Gauls with a stream of soldiers from each side. After days of allowing himself to be tarred as a coward, even by his own men, Sabinus cleverly engineered a simple but resounding victory.

Caesar's own actions after the defeat of the Veneti took him across northern Europe to the northeast corner of Belgica, where he addressed a situation similar to that of Sabinus, that is, an unsubdued foe that was still active in a remote corner of conquered territory. Belgica may have been pacified the previous year, but the Moroni and the Menapii in this area had taken to the woods and marshes to launch hit-and-run, guerrilla-style attacks on the Romans.

Caesar discovered that the swampy, forested terrain favored the defenders. He writes that when the Romans began to fortify their camp, they saw no enemy, but "while our men were dispersed on their respective duties, [the Moroni and the Menapii] suddenly rushed out from all parts of the forest, and made an attack on our men. The latter quickly took up arms and drove them back again to their forests; and having killed a great many, lost a few of their own men while pursuing them too far through those intricate places."

After this Caesar decided upon a scorched earth policy. The legionaries quickly began cutting down the forests and using the logs to build fortifications. At the same time Roman troops caught up with the most vulnerable parts of the Moroni and Menapii social order, capturing their livestock and their supplies. The warriors and their families may have been able to slip away into the brush but could not if they were leading cattle or carrying bushels of corn. When the Romans came upon villages or houses, they burned them. As the rain and cold of winter came on, Caesar was able to withdraw, confident that the Moroni and Menapii had finally gotten his message.

The Roman campaigns in Gaul during 56 BC differed greatly from those of the previous year. While 57 BC had seen operations concentrated mainly in Belgica, those of 56 BC were in far-flung locations across all Gaul.

Another important difference was that the major battles of 56 BC, as well as the major victories, involved Caesar as the strategic commander, though for the most part he was not present tactically as a field commander. Caesar had watched from the shore and had a role in the planning, but the victory in Quiberon Bay belonged to Brutus. In the Cotentin Peninsula it was Sabinus who allowed himself to be humiliated by all sides in order to win his devious but decisive victory. Finally, the conclusive Roman conquest of Aquitania was entirely the work of Publius Crassus and his single reinforced legion.

CHAPTER 10

Across the Rhine

I_F_ 57 BC _WAS_ J_ULIUS_ C_AESAR'S YEAR OF THE_ B_ELGAE, AND_ 56 BC
WAS notable for the conquest of the Veneti and the Aquitani, then
55 BC began as Caesar's year to take the fight across the Rhine into
Germania, and it climaxed with the first Roman cross-channel incursion into Britannia.

In the centuries since, those who have analyzed Caesar's motivations for these operations into lands previously untouched by Roman
legions have theorized that it was as much about politics in Rome
as it was about his lust for conquest. His fellow triumvirs, Pompey
and Marcus Crassus, were at the center of the political action, while
Caesar was far away in the field. In order to maintain and elevate
his own reputation in absentia, he needed to continue to achieve
astounding victories, such as he had in Belgica in 57 BC.

During 55 BC Caesar would also return to his personal involve-
ment in tactical operations, after having largely abstained in 56 BC,
when he had delegated the leadership of key military operations to
his lieutenants, notably Publius Crassus and Decimus Junius Brutus

Albinus. Caesar would now be back at the head of the columns as they marched into combat.

The catalyst for the opening campaign of the year was the cross-Rhine intrusions by Germani. Unlike what had happened in 58 BC, when Ariovistus led the Suebi across the Rhine and snubbed his nose at Caesar, in 55 BC the Germani tribes coming across were being pushed across by the Suebi.

Despite the defeat of Ariovistus by Caesar, the other tribes within Germania found that the Suebi remained a force to be reckoned with. The Romans generally believed the Suebi to be one of the dominant Germanic tribes, or tribal confederations, and one of the more savage.

The most comprehensive Roman study of the Germanic people is the 98 AD book by Publius Cornelius Tacitus, *De Origine et Situ Germanorum*. In it Tacitus writes that the Suebi "occupy more than half of Germania, and are divided into a number of distinct tribes under distinct names, though all generally are called Suebi."

Caesar himself provides a more complete overview of them in his *Commentarii de Bello Gallico*, writing,

The nation of the Suebi is by far the largest and the most warlike nation of all the Germani. They are said to possess a hundred cantons, from each of which they yearly send from their territories for the purpose of war a thousand armed men: the others who remain at home, maintain [both] themselves and those engaged in the expedition. The latter again, in their turn, are in arms the year after: the former remain at home. Thus neither husbandry, nor the art and practice of war are neglected. But among them there exists no private and separate land; nor are they permitted to remain more than one year in one place for the purpose of residence. They do not live much on corn, but subsist for the most part on milk and flesh, and are much [engaged] in hunting; which circumstance must, by the nature of their food, and by their daily exercise and the freedom of their life (for having from boyhood been accustomed to no employment, or discipline, they do nothing at all contrary to their inclination), both promote their strength and render them men of vast stature of body. And to such a habit have they brought themselves, that even in the coldest parts they wear no clothing whatever except skins, by reason of the scantiness of which, a great portion of their body is bare, and besides they bathe in open rivers.

In a more cynical tone, Caesar adds that in their perception of themselves, the skin-wearing Suebi were a people "whom not even the immortal gods can show themselves equal; that there was none at all besides on earth whom they could not conquer." The smaller Germanic tribes east of the Rhine that were bullied by the Suebi appear to have shared Caesar's perception.

Early in 55 BC the Suebi chased the Usipetes and the Tencteri westward into Roman-held Belgica. They passed westward through the marshlands at the mouth of the Rhine and filtered into the lands of the Menapii, whom Caesar had gone to great lengths to subdue during the previous autumn. The Germani—women and children as well as warriors—imposed themselves like unwanted guests, camping on Menapii land and pilfering food.

The same swamps that had made it easy for the Moroni and Menapii to hide from Caesar the previous year created an indistinct border between Belgica and Germania. Indeed, the Rhine has no single mouth. Rather, the Rhine begins in a delta that is part of a much larger delta that also includes the mouths of the Meuse and Scheldt. Therefore it is a region of many rivers, islands, and marshes where delineating a single borderline is complicated.

It would be misleading to suggest that the smaller Germani tribes that crossed this region of indistinct boundaries to raid the Belgae were somehow all victims of Suebi intimidation. Many crossed the delta to steal cattle and plunder from their neighbors even without Suebi provocation. Take, for example, the Sigambri, who lived upriver, between the delta and the mouth of the Moselle. "These men are born for war and raids," Caesar remarks, adding that "no swamp or marsh will stop them."

Even as Caesar's attention was directed to the incidents in the delta, other Germanic infiltrators were being seen farther upriver where the Rhine is more clearly defined. There the Germani encroached upon the Eburones and the Condrusi, Belgic tribes that had submitted to Caesar in 57 BC and were under the protection of the more dominant Treviri, who were allied with the Romans. Emissaries from the Belgic tribes approached Caesar requesting aid because none of them was capable of operations against a foe as powerful as the Suebi. Implicit in their submission to the Romans was that the Romans should protect them from outside threats.

Caesar formed a 5,000-man cavalry force of mainly Gallic horsemen to augment his infantry. They crossed the Meuse River and began marching toward where there was said to be a Germani concentration west of the Rhine, in an area near where the Meuse and the Rhine fragment into their massive delta.

When Caesar was several days' ride from his objective, the Germani sent emissaries to state their position. According to Caesar, he was told that "the Germani neither make war upon the Roman people first, nor do they decline, if they are provoked, to engage with them in arms; for that was the custom of the Germans handed down to them from their forefathers, to resist [invaders by force] and not to avert [invasions] by entreaty...that they had come hither reluctantly, having been expelled from their country. If the Romans were disposed to accept their friendship, they might be serviceable allies to them." They added, goading Caesar, that they felt themselves "inferior to the Suebi alone."

Caesar rebuffed them and kept marching.

When Caesar was 12 miles from their camp, they "earnestly entreated him not to advance any further."

Caesar called their bluff and kept marching.

The Germani, who obviously thought themselves inferior to the Romans as well as the Suebi, asked for a truce.

Caesar agreed to halt his cavalry four miles from them. He writes that he sent his officers to negotiate, noting that he ordered them "not to provoke the enemy to an engagement, [but] if they themselves were assailed, to sustain the attack until [Caesar] came up with the army."

As he explains it, the Germani "made an onset on our men, and soon threw them into disorder. When our men, in their turn, made a stand, they, according to their practice, leaped from their horses to their feet, and stabbing our horses in the belly and overthrowing a great many of our men, put the rest to flight, and drove them forward so much alarmed that they did not desist from their retreat till they had come in sight of our army."

In a rare accounting of Roman and allied casualties, Caesar acknowledges having lost 74 allied cavalrymen in the initial skirmish. After this engagement Caesar "considered that neither ought ambassadors to be received to audience, nor conditions be accepted by him from those who, after having sued for peace by way of stratagem and treachery, had made war without provocation."

Though the Germani assumed that he would tolerate another round of negotiations, Caesar mobilized for a fight, deciding to attack immediately. He had learned that the bulk of the cavalry of the Germani was away on a foraging expedition and they had just 800 horsemen available. He considered waiting until they might return to be "the greatest madness."

Forming his army into three battle lines, Caesar conducted a forced march that took his command straight into the camp of the Germani. Thinking that his Gallic cavalry had been "intimidated by the late skirmish," he placed it in the rear, behind the infantry.

As Caesar describes the battle, "Our soldiers, excited by the treachery of the preceding day, rushed into the camp: such of them as could readily get their arms, for a short time withstood our men, and gave battle among their carts and baggage wagons; but the rest of the people, [consisting] of boys and women (for they had left their country and crossed the Rhine with all their families) began to fly in all directions; in pursuit of whom Caesar sent the cavalry."

The Germani not killed in this battle were forced back across the Rhine. Caesar gives the number of Germani as 430,000 but is unclear as to how many were killed. Obviously exaggerating for his audience at home, he does write that his own troops suffered no one killed in action but adds that a few were wounded. When the news of this battle spread, other tribes that had crossed the Rhine elsewhere also retreated, and Caesar wrote that his war against the Germani west of the river was finished.

Having said this, Caesar pondered the geopolitical reality of the first century BC. Two elements of this reality that everyone understood were that the Rhine was the de facto boundary between Germania and Gaul, and that Rome controlled Gaul. Therefore the

Rhine was the de facto boundary of Roman power. Contemplating this, Caesar noted that if the Germani tested and teased him by slipping across the river, why should he not cross that boundary in the opposite direction as an assertion of Roman power?

As he put it, since the Germani were "so easily urged to go into Gaul," the Germani should "fear for their own territories, when they discovered that the army of the Roman people both could and dared pass the Rhine."

Julius Caesar decided it was time for him to cross the Rhine himself and make a show of force on the eastern shore.

The river at this point was wider than a man could hurl a spear, and at least twice as deep as the height of a man on horseback, and certainly too swift to ford even if it had not been so deep. Caesar might have built barges to transport a contingent of skirmishing cavalry or commandeered rowboats to carry some infantry across. However, he settled upon a show of force that would clearly underscore the superiority of the Romans. He would build a bridge.

Bridging the Rhine was a complex undertaking but one that would show off Roman engineering and organizational skill in the extreme. It was guaranteed to impress the Germani by demonstrating technical expertise well beyond their capability. The spot that he selected was opposite the lands of the Sigambri, about a dozen miles south of where the Moselle enters the Rhine, in the vicinity of the modern German towns of Andernach and Neuwied.

Caesar's bridge was also probably very close to the later site of the famous Ludendorff Bridge at Remagen, a fact which still excites a great deal of interest among military history buffs. It was the only intact bridge across the Rhine as the Allies were making their final push into the Third Reich at the end of World War II, so the capture of the bridge by the US 9th Armored Division in March 1945 was considered a strategic triumph.

It was a complicated process that first involved building pile drivers to sink vertical pilings into the bed of the broad, fast-moving Rhine to support the construction of the bridge. The design even took into account the construction of buffers to prevent the bridge from being damaged by logs floated from upstream to ram the bridge.

Through the years engineers have marveled at Caesar's detailed description of his bridge, studied it, and constructed scale models.

It was an astounding engineering feat, extraordinary for its scale, the quickness of its completion, and the remoteness of its construction site. Of course, all these things pale in comparison with the audacity of the man who envisioned it.

As Caesar writes in *Commentarii de Bello Gallico,* "Within ten days after the timber began to be collected, the whole work was completed, and the whole army led over."

Leaving troops to guard both ends of his bridge, Caesar marched against the Sigambri, who fled into the woods farther east. As he was burning their towns, he was greeted by emissaries from other Germani tribes who offered him tribute and hostages while begging for peace with Rome. He next linked up with warriors from the Ubii, who he mentions as being one of the only Germanic tribes east of the Rhine that had been allied with the Romans before this incursion.

Caesar also received information that the Suebi were preparing for a decisive battle. He writes,

> The Suebi, after they had by means of their scouts found that the bridge was being built, had called a council, according to their custom, and sent orders to all parts of their state to remove from the towns and convey their children, wives, and all their possessions into the woods, and that all who could bear arms should assemble in one place; that the place thus chosen was nearly the centre of those regions which the Suebi possessed; that in this spot they had resolved to await the arrival of the Romans, and give them battle there.

However, as Caesar writes, his objective was not a megabattle against the most powerful of Germanic tribes but, in his words, "to strike fear into the Germani, take vengeance on the Sigambri, and free the Ubii from the invasion of the Suebi."

The Romans withdrew without a fight after just 18 days beyond the Rhine. Caesar had decided that he had "advanced far enough to serve both honor and interest." He was probably also quite hesitant to undertake a major battle, much less a major campaign, with a supply line as tenuous as his bridge. Therefore, to Caesar's "honor and interest," I would add "tactical pragmatism."

As the legions backtracked into Gaul, the great and marvelous bridge was dismantled.

As a student of history, Julius Caesar was probably aware of a similar strategic decision made by Alexander the Great three centuries earlier and many thousands of miles to the east. Alexander had conquered Persia and had marched his armies all the way across modern Afghanistan and Tajikistan to reach the river now known as the Syr Darya. Across it lay the vast steppes of Central Asia, or Scythia. Rather than continuing his march into modern Kazakhstan in an attempt to defeat the Scythians, Alexander did as the Persians had done before him. He designated the natural barrier of the Syr Darya his northern frontier—and built fortress cities, including Alexandria Eschate, meaning Alexandria the Farthest, to defend it. In 329 BC, before he left for other conquests, Alexander conducted a series of aggressive military patrols and search-and-destroy operations beyond the river.

The strategic objective of Alexander's brief cross-river campaign against the Scythians was exactly the same as Caesar's 18-day sojourn beyond the Rhine. Neither general had the intention to stay, but in both cases the enemy learned which natural barrier the conqueror intended to defend as his boundary.

As natural boundaries go, the Rhine was substantial for any army operating in the first century BC. Indeed, the Rhine was still seen as a substantial barrier by the Allied armies two millennia later in World War II. In March 1945 the capture of an intact bridge across the Rhine at Remagen (about 25 miles downriver from Caesar's bridge) was considered to be an accomplishment of immense strategic importance.

CHAPTER 11

Mysterious Britannia

OF ALL THE NATURAL BOUNDARIES IN EUROPEAN POLITICAL AND MILITARY history, few can compare to the English Channel. Across it lay the mysterious land where few, if any, Romans had ever ventured.

For the Romans of the first century BC, Britain, the place they called Britannia, was a distant, enigmatic, and untouchable place. Meanwhile, in the Roman world view, the English Channel was not a mere channel, but part of Oceanus, the vast body of water which they, like the Greeks, understood to surround all of the known world. Because this mysterious land lay in Oceanus, and therefore beyond the confines of the known world, it could be said that Britannia was thought of as being *another world*.

As Cassius Dio writes in his *Historia Romana* (*Roman History*), "To the very earliest of the Greeks and Romans it was not even known to exist, while to their descendants it was a matter of dispute whether it was a continent or an island; and accounts of it have been written from both points of view by many who knew nothing about it, because they had not seen it with their own eyes nor heard about it from the natives with their own ears, but indulged in surmises."

For Julius Caesar it was a place populated by Celtic tribes related ethnically and culturally to the Celtic tribes that were his foes in northern Gaul. Britannia was less mysterious to him because, while he was operating on the Atlantic and English Channel coastlines in northern Gaul, he had occasionally made contact with traders and fishers who lived there. While many Romans considered it to be almost a mythical place, for Caesar it was a place whose white cliffs he could actually see from Gaul—on a clear day.

However, even after campaigning on the south side of the English Channel for three seasons, Caesar still knew little about Britannia. In *Commentarii de Bello Gallico,* he explains that even after speaking with people who had been there, he "could learn neither what was the size of the island, nor what or how numerous were the nations which inhabited it, nor what system of war they followed, nor what customs they used, nor what harbors were convenient for a great number of large ships."

But Britannia was an object of great strategic interest to Caesar. So long as the unconquered Celts in Britannia crossed the English Channel, giving aid and comfort to the conquered Celts of coastal Brittany and Normandy, Caesar had a reason to go. As he writes in *Commentarii de Bello Gallico,* "In almost all the wars with the Gauls succors had been furnished to our enemy from that country."

As he considered Britannia, he even had the audacity to imagine that one day there should be a permanent Roman presence there, although his plans for 55 BC did not involve going there to stay. Like his venture into Germania, it would be only a show of force.

Another comparison with World War II is germane. The Allied strategic objectives in 1944 were the same as Caesar's strategic objectives in 55 BC: to cross the English Channel and establish a military expeditionary force on the opposite side. With the Allies the place was Normandy on the south side. For Caesar it was Britannia on the north.

Although it was late in the campaigning season, and the weather around the channel was growing worse by the day, Caesar was undaunted.

Intelligence was vital (just as it would prove to be in 1944). To gather the necessary information, he dispatched Gaius Volusenus Quadratus, a tribune in Legio XII under Servius Galba, to take a ship and conduct a weeklong reconnaissance of the Britannia coastline in the area called Cantium, now Kent. Volusenus scouted the shore, roughly between the present-day towns of Hythe and Sandwich, looking for a likely landing beach.

In the meantime Caesar ordered that 80 transport vessels from the fleet he had used for operations against the Veneti in 56 BC should be assembled on the coast to carry two legions, Legio VII and Caesar's favored Legio X, across the channel.

Although ships designed for coastal rowing were at a disadvantage in the rough waters of the channel, the Romans made it. The location of Caesar's intended landing was probably in the vicinity of Dover, but when he observed "the forces of the enemy drawn up in arms on all the hills [the White Cliffs of Dover]," he ordered the fleet to coast several miles eastward. The exact landing site is unknown, but it was probably on the broad, sandy beach near the modern town of Walmer. Julius Caesar notes that it was "over against an open and level shore" that he first set foot in Britannia.

The landing did not go unopposed. Caesar writes that "the barbarians, upon perceiving the design of the Romans, sent forward their cavalry and charioteers, a class of warriors of whom it is their practice to make great use in their battles, and following with the rest of their forces, endeavored to prevent our men landing." But the Romans were having difficulty with the landing for another reason.

Although Roman civil engineering on the Rhine was superb, the same cannot be said for Roman naval planners' preparations for the landings in Britannia. Someone should have realized that ships designed for deep-water operations, with a substantial part of their hull beneath the waterline, couldn't take the troops all the way to the beach. In 1944 some Allied landing craft got caught on obstacles, forcing the troops to wade or swim ashore, but in 55 BC all the legionaries were forced to stagger through sticky sand while being struck by neck-high waves and British arrows.

As Caesar writes,

> Our soldiers, in places unknown to them, with their hands embarrassed, oppressed with a large and heavy weight of armor, had at the same time to leap from the ships, stand amid the waves, and encounter the enemy; whereas they, either on dry ground, or advancing a little way into the water, free in all their limbs in places thoroughly known to them, could confidently throw their weapons and spur on their horses, which were accustomed to this kind of service. Dismayed by these circumstances and altogether untrained in this mode of battle, our men did not all exert the same vigor and eagerness which they had been wont to exert in engagements on dry ground.

Fortunately, Caesar had the presence of mind to have his supporting warships begin a slings-and-arrows bombardment of the advancing Britanni, driving them back from the shore.

Meanwhile the standard-bearer from Legio X rallied the men to follow him, and the Romans staggered up the beach. As soon as the bulk of the legionaries managed to get their footing on dry ground, they counterattacked and drove the Britanni from the beachhead. It was, however, impossible to pursue them as the 18 ships carrying the Roman cavalry had lagged behind and did not make their landing in time. Indeed, most of these had turned around and returned to Gaul.

Having narrowly escaped a rout, Caesar claimed victory.

Within a short time British emissaries approached the Romans. A conference was held about four days later, which Caesar interpreted as a British capitulation, writing that "the chiefs assembled from all quarters, and proceeded to surrender themselves and their states."

It was not by, any means, the end of the conflict.

The Romans held their beachhead but never marched inland in force. Foraging parties that went into the interior were ambushed and badly mauled. Even Caesar acknowledged that his men were at a disadvantage in combat against the mounted Britanni in the rolling, wooded hills of Cantium.

As Caesar later wrote, describing this land in *Commentarii de Bello Gallico,* "The interior portion of Britannia is inhabited by those of whom they say that it is handed down by tradition that they were born in the island itself...the maritime portion by those who had passed over from the country of the Belgae for the purpose of plunder and making war....The most civilized of all these nations are they who inhabit Cantium, which is entirely a maritime district, nor do they differ much from the Gallic customs."

Though Caesar could spin the reaction of the Britanni to the landing as a Roman success, he could not spin the worsening weather.

As Caesar writes, "The storm began to dash the ships of burden which were riding at anchor against each other; nor was any means afforded our men of either managing them or of rendering any service. A great many ships having been wrecked, inasmuch as the rest, having lost their cables, anchors, and other tackling, were unfit for sailing, a great confusion, as would necessarily happen, arose throughout the army; for there were no other ships in which they could be conveyed back, and all things which are of service in repairing vessels were wanting."

At last Caesar decided that lingering in Britannia without adequate provisions was an untenable position. Preparations were made to recross the English Channel in the boats that were still available.

In an epilogue to the first Roman incursion into Britannia, he adds simply that "corn for the winter had not been provided in those places, because it was understood by all that they would certainly winter in Gaul."

Caesar returned to Gaul only to find that while he was away, the tribes of northeast Belgica had revolted. Now back in his element, and with his full army at his disposal, he acted decisively. He sent Titus Atius Labienus, in command of Legio VII and Legio X, against the Morini, who, "as they had no place to which they might retreat, on account of the drying up of their marshes (which they had availed themselves of as a place of refuge the preceding year)," were totally defeated.

Meanwhile, Caesar dispatched Quintus Titurius Sabinus and Lucius Aurunculeius Cotta to lead legions into the territories of the

Menapii, where the Romans "laid waste all their lands, cut down their corn and burned their houses."

And so 55 BC came to a close. Caesar was still the master of Belgica, and he had campaigned in both Germania and Britannia—beyond where anyone had previously led a legion without being defeated. Though he had withdrawn from both, he had done so on his own terms without suffering a defeat. Thus he was able to masterfully spin his campaigns as victories.

When the news, crafted by Caesar himself, reached Rome, the Senate decreed a 20-day Supplicatio (Thanksgiving)—five days more than he had received in 57 BC. Though he was in winter quarters far from home, Julius Caesar was still Rome's number one hero and favorite son.

CHAPTER 12

Back to Britannia

THE SUPPLICATIO CELEBRATED IN ROME AT THE CLOSE OF CAESAR'S 55 BC campaigns confirmed his greatness. The man himself also may well have believed all the great things they said about him in the salons and on the Senate floor. However, nobody knew the tactical shortcomings of his expedition to Britannia better than Caesar.

Except for a brief trip to Illyricum to deal with a short-lived insurgency, he spent his winter in Cisalpine Gaul, not basking in his glory but pondering his mistakes—for a practical reason. He was plotting his return to Britannia in 54 BC, and he was examining all the things he had done wrong, so that he could do them right.

Should he again have a late start as the winds of autumn were beginning to blow?

No, he would embark for Britannia at the start of summer.

Would he again use boats designed to Roman specifications for the deep and placid waters of the Mediterranean?

No, he would use shallow draft boats built to the specifications of his old adversaries, the Veneti, who knew and understood these waters. Indeed, he had gotten the shipbuilding activities underway even before the end of 55 BC. As he writes in *Commentarii de Bello Gallico*, the ships were "broader than those which we use in other seas...constructed for lightness and expedition, to which object their lowness contributes greatly."

Instead of the expeditionary force of two legions, this time he would land in force, with five legions, more than half his total army. The cavalry hadn't arrived last time, but this year he would give high priority to seeing that the horsemen made it. In *Commentarii de Bello Gallico* Caesar mentions various numbers between 2,000 and 4,000, mainly Gallic horsemen. Finally, in 55 BC he had depended on foraging, but in 54 BC he assembled a sizable number of supply vessels to augment his landing ships.

Because of his plan to take most of his army to Britannia, Caesar had to concern himself with potential unrest among his Gallic subjects. In order to ensure continued compliance, he decided to take selected Gallic leaders with him, more or less as hostages.

Notable among those he planned to take with him was Dumnorix of the Aedui, who had been a loyal Caesar follower since the early campaigns of 58 BC. However, as Caesar writes in *Commentarii de Bello Gallico*, it turned out that because Dumnorix was "unaccustomed to sailing, he feared the sea," and he was "prevented by divine admonitions" from leaving Gaul. Caesar adds that Dumnorix accused him of "insane designs to be proceeding further and further." Being confrontational with a man of Caesar's power was a serious mistake. Caesar decided that he could no longer trust his old friend and had him killed. Caesar took Dumnorix's Aedui cavalry to Britannia.

Finally, Julius Caesar left Labienus in command of the Gaul garrison with three legions and 2,000 cavalrymen; they embarked from the Roman port of Portus Itius (thought to be near Boulogne, France). His invasion fleet numbered 800 ships, including 28 warships, as well as transports for men, horses, and supplies.

Despite the size of the force, this was not to be a precursor to Caesar's long-range ideas about a permanent Roman presence in Britannia. As had been the case the year before, Caesar's purpose was a show of force to demonstrate Roman military power.

After battling difficult tides overnight, Caesar's oarsmen began landing men in Britannia after nearly 24 hours at sea. They made landfall on the same site where they had come ashore the preceding summer, because, writes Caesar, "there was the best landing-place."

Unlike the reception that greeted Caesar in 55 BC, not a single Briton was on hand to oppose the vast landing. Caesar surmised that they were "alarmed by the great number of our ships [and] had quitted the coast and concealed themselves among the higher points."

The new landing boats also worked out well. The previous year the deepwater boats had been hung up offshore, and the troops had to climb out and wade through the deep breakers. This year the shallow-draft boats worked as planned, allowing the Roman troops to remain afloat as far onto the beaches as the waves reached.

Caesar moved quickly—he had had plenty of time through the previous winter to plan his course of action. He left Quintus Atrius in command at the beachhead with ten cohorts and 300 cavalry to guard the invasion fleet and marched the remainder of the troops inland as soon as they could be assembled. They traveled north, toward the marshlands surrounding the Thames Estuary, the mouth of Britannia's great river, the Tamesis (Thames). Caesar probably knew about it from having debriefed British prisoners, and set the population centers in this vicinity as an objective of his march.

Caesar identifies the warlord in command of the Britanni at this time as Cassivellaunus, a chieftain who is also mentioned in ancient British sources and who is listed by Geoffrey of Monmouth in his twelfth-century *Historia Regum Britanniae* (*History of the Kings of Britain*). Caesar believed that the warring factions of the Britanni patched up their differences after the first Roman invasion in 55 BC and formed a unified command under Cassivellaunus. Caesar writes, "Greatly alarmed by our arrival, the Britons had placed him over the whole war and the conduct of it."

Caesar himself traveled a dozen miles inland the first night and began observing the Britanni preparing for battle. The Romans resisted initial probes by Britanni cavalry, pursuing the enemy to a position that Caesar describes as "admirably fortified by nature and by art, which, as it seemed, they had before prepared on account of a civil war; for all entrances to it were shut up by a great number of felled trees."

Legio VII attacked the fortifications, driving the Britanni back, but Caesar halted the pursuit because it was getting dark and the weather was turning foul. He did not want his troops thrashing about in unfamiliar terrain at night and during a storm. At daybreak he was preparing the infantry and cavalry to continue the pursuit when he received word from the beachhead that during the storm "almost all the ships were dashed to pieces and cast upon the shore, because neither the anchors and cables could resist."

Given the previous year's crippling weather problems, it had to have been the most bitter of ironies for Caesar to contemplate being so badly harmed by a storm less than a week after this year's landings. Of all the changes that he had made in readiness for the second year's campaign, Caesar had apparently failed to adequately prepare for nature's wrath.

Caesar recalled his cavalry patrols, ordered his planned advance against the Britanni to stand down, and hurried back to survey the damage. He observed that about 40 vessels had to be written off as total losses, but that represented only about 1 or 2 percent of his total troop transports, and the remainder seemed "capable of being repaired with much labor." He ordered this work to begin immediately and sent a messenger back to Labienus in Gaul, ordering him to begin construction of additional vessels.

When Caesar returned to his troops at the front, and resumed his march toward the Thames, he quickly encountered the Britanni, who were ready to fight. As the Romans marched through the woods and hills, they were drawn into skirmishes with Britanni horsemen, who often fell back, drawing the legionaries into ambushes.

Caesar, who usually didn't mention Roman casualties, complained about losing men in these actions. An exasperated Caesar writes,

In the whole of this method of fighting since the engagement took place under the eyes of all and before the camp, it was perceived that our men, on account of the weight of their arms, inasmuch as they could neither pursue [the enemy when] retreating, nor dare quit their standards, were little suited to this kind of enemy; that the horse also fought with great danger, because they [the Britanni] generally retreated even designedly, and, when they had drawn off our men a short distance from the legions, leaped from their chariots and fought on foot in unequal [and to them advantageous] battle.

Caesar had earlier described the people of Cantium as the "most civilized" in Britannia, but he described the island's "inland inhabitants" as quite different. He writes in *Commentarii de Bello Gallico* that they did not "sow corn, but live on milk and flesh, and are clad with skins."

In *Commentarii de Bello Gallico* Caesar paints a particularly vivid picture of the warriors whom he faced. "All the Britons," he writes, "dye themselves with wood, which occasions a bluish color, and thereby have a more terrible appearance in fight. They wear their hair long, and have every part of their body shaved except their head and upper lip."

The fierce attacks by such fearsome warriors were unnerving to the legionaries, but gradually discipline and training prevailed, and the Romans were able to exploit the tactics the Britanni were using against them. Shortly after the Britanni brazenly and suddenly attacked three legions and all the Roman cavalry, which Caesar had sent on a foraging mission under the legatus Gaius Trebonius, the tables were turned.

"Our men making an attack on them vigorously, repulsed them," he writes. "Nor did they cease to pursue them until the [cavalry], relying on relief, as they saw the legions behind them, drove the enemy precipitately before them, and slaying a great number of them, did not give them the opportunity either of rallying, or halting, or leaping from their chariots. Immediately after this retreat, the auxiliaries, who had assembled from all sides, departed."

The Romans marched north and west, reaching the Thames upriver from its mouth at a place where it was broad and difficult to ford. Across the river and some distance away lay the territory of Cassivellaunus himself, in what is now Hertfordshire. Caesar writes that "numerous forces of the enemy were marshaled on the other bank of the river; the bank also was defended by sharp stakes fixed in front, and stakes of the same kind fixed under the water were covered by the river."

Although the Thames was shoulder deep, Caesar ordered an immediate attack. The speed of the crossing, which was preceded by the Roman cavalry, apparently caught the Britanni off guard and compelled them to retreat en masse into the woods.

The Roman reaction earlier in the campaign would have been to break off individual contingents to pursue the fragmented army of the enemy. However, experience had now taught the legionaries that such actions were usually turned against the Romans in ambushes. Therefore Caesar ordered the legions to stay together. Now that he was into the heartland of Cassivellaunus, he knew that he could do more damage by laying waste to the fields and by burning the villages of the Britanni.

The process of scorching enemy land did not often win friends, but in Caesar's experience it often neutralized foes. Caesar notes that at this point in the campaign, a sizable number of tribes approached him offering to surrender and provide the Romans with provisions. He specifically lists the Ancalites, Bibroci, Cassi, Cenimagni, and Segontiaci, as well as the Trinobantes, who he mentions as having earlier sent emissaries to meet him in Gaul and who were already under his protection.

The Romans pressed on, marching northward toward the stronghold of Cassivellaunus, which is thought to have been in the vicinity of the town of Wheathampstead. Caesar describes the place as "defended by woods and morasses, [with] a very large number of men and of cattle" in anticipation of a siege. In fact, there was no siege at all. The Romans attacked from two sides, quickly overwhelmed the defenses, and picked off the enemy warriors as they tried to escape.

Cassivellaunus schemed one last, desperate strike against Caesar. His plan was to make an end run against the Romans by attacking their base camp on the Channel coast. Enlisting the support of other warlords to carry this out, he had hoped to destroy or at least damage the Roman fleet. Had it worked, it would have been considered strategic brilliance at its best, but the plan was flawed by his having delegated the operation to those who lacked the skill to pull it off.

When Cassivellaunus learned that this assault had failed, and that his troops had suffered high losses, he sent emissaries to Caesar offering to surrender. Under the terms of this capitulation Cassivellaunus agreed to submit hostages, pay an annual tribute to the Romans, and never to wage war upon Caesar's friends, the Trinobantes, or their king, Mandubratius.

By now, with the autumn storm season approaching, Caesar was eager to return to Gaul. Traveling in two waves because they had taken so many Britanni prisoners, the Romans managed to make the channel crossing without losing any ships.

Caesar never set foot in Britannia again. He may have considered his mission to have been accomplished, or he may have been too preoccupied with later events and activities to repeat such a massive undertaking on so precarious a shore.

Though the support from the Britanni for Gallic and Belgic insurgency represented his tactical excuse for going to Britannia, his strategic reasoning clearly involved the greater glory of Rome.

Other motivations have also been advanced. Suetonius offers an unusual theory, writing, "They say that he was led to invade Britannia by the hope of getting pearls, and that in comparing their size he sometimes weighed them with his own hand; that he was always a most enthusiastic collector of gems."

However, what drove Caesar to go where no Roman army had gone before was clearly a mix of his lust for magnificence and the need to project Roman strategic power to the edges of the earth.

Julius Caesar had imagined a permanent Roman presence in Britannia, and he may have planned that his alliance with the Trinobantes was a first step toward a third cross-channel operation within the next few years to establish a permanent garrison. As it was, Caesar would never return, and it would be nearly a century before his countrymen, during the rule of the emperor Claudius, returned to stay.

CHAPTER 13

Threats from within Gaul

JULIUS CAESAR RETURNED TO THE CONTINENT IN THE AUTUMN OF 54 BC having reached the geographical high-water mark of his campaigns. He had defeated the Britanni in Britannia and the Germani in Germania.

However, as he set foot back in Gaul, the dominions that he had conquered and subjugated during the four previous years were becoming restive. Poor harvests, combined with Roman confiscation of foodstuffs, would soon lead to a series of revolts.

Caesar's habit had been to put his legions into winter quarters in various places in Gaul to function essentially as an occupation force, though in past years little policing had been required. For the winter of 54–53 BC he placed three legions in Belgica and one each among the Esubii, Morini, Nervii, and Remi. The last was adjacent to the territories of the Treviri, which were in the Moselle River Valley and included the site of the later Roman city of Treverorum, which is now Trier, Germany.

Caesar detailed Quintus Titurius Sabinus, victor in the 56 BC Normandy campaign, and Lucius Aurunculeius Cotta to command the legion stationed among the Eburones, who occupied the area between the Meuse and the Rhine north of the Treviri. This would be the flash point of the revolts in the winter of 54–53 BC. The leaders of the Eburones, Ambiorix and Cativolcus, whose relations with the Romans had previously been amiable, were now contemplating insurrection.

About two weeks after Sabinus and Cotta arrived to fortify their winter quarters, the unrest reached a boil. The Eburones attacked and killed a contingent of legionaries who had gone outside the walls while gathering firewood. Then the Eburones attacked the Roman fort itself. Though they were driven off, they had certainly gotten the attention of the Romans, who went on high alert.

A conference with Ambiorix was arranged, and the leader of the Eburones appeared cordial. He explained that he really wanted to maintain good relations with the Romans, but he painted a dire picture of a dangerous threat welling up among the Remi just across the Rhine. With this in mind he cautioned Sabinus and Cotta to relocate their camp to a safer and more easily defended location.

The two Roman leaders went away to debate the merits of this proposal. Sabinus was, as Caesar writes in *Commentarii de Bello Gallico,* "convinced that the advice was given by Ambiorix, not as an enemy, but as most friendly." Cotta disagreed but was finally persuaded to go along with Sabinus. The following day they ordered the legionaries to pack up and move out.

As the Romans were marching through a broad valley, they were suddenly attacked by Eburones, who controlled the high ground in all directions. It was, as Caesar calls it, "a place exceedingly disadvantageous to our men. [The terrain's effects on the ensuing battle] turned out unfortunately; for it both diminished the hope of our soldiers and rendered the enemy more eager for the fight" because possession of the high ground was favorable for the Eburones.

From one point in their defensive line the Romans counterattacked. As the Eburones fell back, the Romans pursued, but this left a weakness in the line that other Eburones quickly exploited.

During a momentary lull in the fighting the Romans called for a truce and for a conference with Ambiorix. The Eubrones agreed, so Sabinus and several centurions went up to meet with Ambiorix, putting down their arms as they approached him. However, the Eburones responded by shouting "Victory!" and killing Sabinus. Ambiorix then led his troops in a final assault against the Roman lines. Cotta was killed in action, along with a sizable number of his men, during a bloody battle that lasted until nightfall. A handful of legionaries managed to get away into the woods under cover of darkness, but most of the Roman contingent was slaughtered.

Jubilant at having rendered unto the Romans one of their worst defeats in Gaul, Ambiorix immediately tried to keep up his momentum by encouraging the Aduatuci and the Nervii to revolt against Roman rule. He insisted, as Caesar recalls, "that they should not throw away the opportunity of liberating themselves forever and of punishing the Romans for those wrongs which they had received from them."

The Nervii seized the opportunity to reverse the humiliation of their 57 BC defeat by Caesar. With the aid of Ambiorix and the Eburones, the Nervii attacked the legion commanded by Quintus Cicero, which was wintering in their territory. Unlike Sabinus and Cotta, who were caught in the open, Cicero was in a fortified position, and his legion held off the initial attack. Overnight the Romans built siege works and thwarted another assault the following day.

As he had with Sabinus and Cotta, Ambiorix called a conference, telling Cicero the same story of the Germanic uprising and insisting that it was in Cicero's best interests to withdraw his legion from its precarious and easily surrounded winter quarters in the heartland of the Nervii.

Cicero gave Ambiorix a message similar to one that another general would deliver when surrounded in almost the same geographical location in another winter in the middle of World War II. In December 1944 US Brigadier General Anthony McAuliffe of the 101st Airborne Division was surrounded by German forces in Bastogne, Belgium, during the Battle of the Bulge. Given an ultimatum by German general Heinrich von Lüttwitz to surrender his untenable position, McAuliffe replied simply, "Nuts."

Cicero, as the brother of the famous Roman orator, Marcus Cicero, may have replied more eloquently, but the answer was essentially identical.

Just as McAuliffe sent word to the Third Army's commander, General George Patton, requesting support, Cicero sent messengers to Caesar, but for the moment Cicero was on his own.

The Romans, who were not used to seeing the Gauls as engineers, were amazed when the Belgae managed to quickly surround the Roman winter quarters with a rampart, having learned the art of earthworks from Roman engineers captured in earlier battles. Caesar describes it as being 11 feet high, and ten miles in circumference.

A week into the battle the Belgae launched their final assault, preceding it with a shower of hot rocks and other implements designed to set fire to Roman supplies and the thatched structures inside the camp. Despite the ensuing conflagration in their midst and a fierce Belgic assault, the Romans held.

Cicero's messenger finally managed to get through to Caesar, who assembled a 400-man cavalry contingent and marched toward the siege himself. He also ordered three legions in various corners of Gaul to march in relief of Cicero immediately. However, Titus Labienus, commanding the legion wintering among the Treviri, convinced Caesar that his legion should remain in place, lest the Treviri decide to join the revolt. Indeed, the Treviri warrior leader Indutiomarus was an outspoken supporter of the Belgic insurrection and a serious threat to the pro-Roman Treviri leader Cingetorix, who was coincidentally also his son-in-law.

When word of Caesar's approach reached the scene of Cicero's siege, the Romans were elated, and the Belgae were apprehensive. They pulled back from the siege, rallying to face Caesar in battle.

As Caesar writes in *Commentarii de Bello Gallico,* his two legions plus auxiliaries, "scarcely 7,000 men," were faced by an enemy force of 60,000 and thus outnumbered significantly. The figures were almost certainly exaggerated by Caesar, but the Belgic force was formidable. Aware that the siege against Cicero had been lifted, Caesar halted his force to prepare a fortified position from which to face the enemy.

At first the Roman horsemen engaged in cavalry skirmishes, then withdrew, luring the Belgae into a trap set by Caesar. The trap was closed, the battle joined, and the Belgae badly battered. It was time for the Romans to go in pursuit, but Caesar cautiously held back from chasing the enemy into the deep woods, fearing his own men would be ambushed.

Caesar instead broke off the battle and resumed his march toward Cicero's position, linking up with him by the end of the day. Caesar commended the besieged contingent and their commander for valor, then learned of the deaths of Sabinus and Cotta.

The victory over the Nervii and their allies turned out to have other positive results for the Romans. A messenger from Labienus arrived to tell Caesar that the anti-Roman Treviri under Indutiomarus, who had been planning a revolt, had backed off and stood down.

Caesar had prevailed, but it had not been easy. His legions had suffered some tense moments and a terrible massacre, and Caesar had been compelled to fight during the harsh northern European winter, a difficult chore that Roman generals tried to avoid if they could. As for Ambiorix, he got away and managed to maintain a low profile for the next several months.

Though Caesar had turned a near disaster into a victory for the Roman occupation of Gaul, the winter of 54–53 BC was a trial for him.

The Romans had curbed open rebellion, but rumblings and murmurings were everywhere. Late in the winter the intra-Treviri acrimony between Indutiomarus and Cingetorix boiled over into a civil war. Indutiomarus and his faction prevailed, confiscating Cingetorix's property and relieving him of a tribal leadership role. Indutiomarus then, following the tactics of Ambiorix from the previous year, surrounded the camp of Labienus. The Roman legatus detected an opening in the Treviri siege line and sent a cavalry patrol out to take the offensive. Caught off guard, Indutiomarus pulled back. But before he could regroup his forces, Indutiomarus was killed while fording a river. His army, suddenly without a leader, pulled back from the siege—but only to regroup for another try several weeks later.

The year 53 BC would by necessity be Caesar's year of the defensive. The winter unrest had shown him that that his dominions in Gaul might be starting to crumble, and he was determined to prevent that. He increased the strength of his army to ten legions and set out to quell potential insurrections.

Based on his experiences during the winter, he singled out tribes that had actively rebelled or that had grumbled the loudest. His operations, which began even before the spring thaw, were swift and proactive, hitting targets before they had a chance to undertake their own spring offensives. Caesar's operations were also fierce and brutally preemptive. He attacked the Nervii and then moved on the Senones and the Carnutes, who lived in the area of north-central France roughly between the Seine and Loire Rivers.

Caesar next returned to the Rhine delta, that nagging problem area, marching at the head of five lightly equipped legions. As they had three years earlier, the delta tribes were infiltrating across the indistinct boundaries of the delta, where they screened their movements with the marshes and dense woods. With each of these tribes Caesar laid waste to their property, killed their livestock, took hostages, and generally removed the infrastructure that could support a society at war. By attacking them aggressively and unexpectedly early in the season, he had caught them before they had an opportunity to mobilize.

Caesar's next move took him south, where Labienus still occupied his stronghold in the heart of Treviri country. Although Indutiomarus was dead, his anti-Roman faction still dominated the tribe, and the Treviri were preparing to resume the fray. Furthermore, they had elicited a promise of support from the Germanic tribes across the Rhine, including Caesar's old nemesis, the Suebi. When Labienus figured out that the enemy was waiting for reinforcements, and these would soon arrive, he decided to act before either Caesar or the Suebi could arrive.

As Caesar describes his legatus's preparations in *Commentarii de Bello Gallico*, "After leaving a guard of five cohorts for the baggage, [Labienus] advances against the enemy with 25 cohorts and a large body of cavalry, and, leaving the space of a mile between them, fortifies his camp. There was between Labienus and the enemy a river difficult to cross, and with steep banks: this neither did he himself design to cross, nor did he suppose the enemy would cross it."

This was the opening step in what Labienus planned as a deception that he hoped would become a trap. That night he ordered the camp to be moved "with greater noise and confusion than was usual with the Roman people. By these means he makes his departure [appear] like a retreat. These things, also, since the camps were so near, are reported to the enemy by scouts before daylight."

The Treviri, naturally believing that Labienus had decided on a quick pullout under cover of darkness because he feared the arrival of the Germani, took the bait. They plunged into the river, racing to attack the retreating Romans—even though the Treviri would have to wade out of the water and climb a steep embankment on the opposite side.

With the Treviri in such an awkward position, the Romans turned, as Labienus had planned, to meet them. Instead of chasing a frightened foe, the Treviri found themselves on the receiving end of Roman spears with their backs to the river, crushed in a resounding defeat.

The whole Treviri insurgency abruptly collapsed on those muddy cliffs. As Caesar summarizes, "The Germani, who were coming to the aid of the Treviri, having been informed of their flight, retreated to their homes. The relations of Indutiomarus, who had been the promoters of the revolt, accompanying them, quitted their own state with them. The supreme power and government were delivered to Cingetorix, whom we have stated to have remained firm in his allegiance [to Rome] from the commencement."

Although the Germani retreated quickly, Caesar decided to once again cross the Rhine. His reason was not simply to teach the Suebi a lesson for having dared to consider aiding the Treviri—though that was obviously part of it—but to show all the Germani that the Roman ability to execute Rhine crossings was no fluke.

In *Commentarii de Bello Gallico* Caesar devotes much less space to describing this crossing than he did to his 55 BC bridge. He mentions that it was a short distance above the previous bridge, and he adds that it was completed "in a few days by the great exertion of the soldiers." That he doesn't go into any detail regarding the design suggests that it was essentially the same design as the earlier one.

As before, Caesar left a strong guard at either end of the bridge and proceeded into the interior, looking for a fight. When he made contact with his friends the Ubii, he learned that the Suebi were preparing for battle, "drawing all their forces into one place, and [were] giving orders to those nations which are under their government to send auxiliaries of infantry and of cavalry."

Caesar notes that they were preparing for battle deep inside their territory at a place he describes as Silva Bacenis (Beech Forest), which may have been as far east as the Elbe River. Because of this Caesar reconsidered this adventure, wary of penetrating too deeply into enemy territory, and halted his advance. As he pulled back and recrossed his bridge, Caesar decided not to completely dismantle it this time. So as to "not altogether relieve the barbarians from the fear of his return," he left 200 feet of it, and "at the extremity of the bridge raised towers of four stories, and stationed a guard of twelve cohorts for the purpose of defending the bridge, and strengthened the place with considerable fortifications."

Caesar's plan now was to continue scorching the earth of the Belgic tribes in an effort to cripple them and prevent the insurgency of the previous winter. With autumn approaching he wanted them to be spending their time scrounging for food and shelter, not sitting around with full bellies and plotting revolution.

Unfortunately, the Romans had not so much crushed their opposition into submission as they had smashed them into many small fragments that *defied* submission. The defeat of the Treviri by Labienus had been the last major battle of 53 BC. Caesar's campaign had now shifted from one of large-scale battles to a classical counterinsurgency, in which a large field army must fight a guerrilla war against small bands of opponents in difficult terrain. As he writes, there was now "no regular army, nor a town, nor a garrison which could defend itself by arms; but the people were scattered in all directions. Where either a hidden valley, or a woody spot, or a difficult morass furnished any hope of protection or of security to any one.... These places were known to those who dwelt in the neighborhood, and the matter demanded great attention."

Labienus proceeded north toward coastal Belgica, west of the Rhine delta with three legions, while Gaius Trebonius marched with three legions "to lay waste that district which lies contiguous to the Aduatuci." With the remainder of the army Caesar headed into the hinterlands of the homeland of the Eburones, the dark woods of the Ardennes highlands, which he describes as the largest forest in Gaul.

As in the early spring offensives against the Nervii, Senones, and Carnutes, Caesar moved quickly, maintaining the element of surprise to keep the Belgae off guard. One by one Caesar's men attacked remote villages and encampments with little or no warning. Again, the Romans found themselves vulnerable, not to enemy armies but to small raiding parties. Like the Partisans would fight the invading Germans in this same country in World War II, these raiders preyed upon Roman foragers and support personnel with little or no warning.

During these search-and-destroy operations, Caesar reports happily that the Romans happened "by a remarkable chance" to stumble into the camp of Ambiorix himself in the remote corner of the Ardennes where he had been hiding for the past several months.

However, luck and terrain were on Ambiorix's side, just as they were for Osama bin Laden in the mountains of Afghanistan when he barely eluded the US Army's Special Forces in 2001.

Caesar relates that as the Romans attacked Ambiorix's house, "one of his followers mounted him on a horse; the woods sheltered him as he fled. Thus fortune tended much both toward his encountering and his escaping danger.... Fortune accomplishes much, not only in other matters, but also in the art of war." Nevertheless the Romans did manage to capture Ambiorix's chariots and horses, and "every implement of war which he was accustomed to have about him."

Caesar ran down leads and searched far and wide. In the process he became a scourge of the Eburones.

Their other leader, Cativolcus, who was an old man by this time, had not been able to achieve the kind of reputation that Ambiorix had during the 53 BC campaign. Cativolcus wound up cursing his former colleague, not for usurping all the glory but for bringing the wrath of Caesar down upon the Eburones. As Caesar writes, "Now worn out by age, [Cativolcus] was unable to endure the fatigue either of war or flight." As the year neared its end, Cativolcus committed suicide by eating the foliage of the yew tree, which is toxic in large doses.

As the first snowflakes drifted through the trees in the deep forests, and as Caesar wound up his operations and headed back to Italy for the winter, Ambiorix slipped away. He managed to escape east of the Rhine, never to be seen again. Despite so ignominious a departure, he became a popular folk legend among the Belgae, and he remains a hero in Belgium to this day.

Gaius Julius Caesar served as both consul and proconsul in the Roman Republic before undertaking the military campaigns which transformed him into a conquering hero of immense proportions, and which permanently transformed the map of Europe. (Author's collection)

Gnaeus Pompeius Magnus, or Pompey the Great, was one of the Roman Republic's towering figures, and Caesar's bitterest rival. He served with Caesar in the First Triumvirate, married Caesar's daughter, and fought him in the bloody civil war. (Author's collection)

The father of Gaius Julius Caesar, also named Gaius Julius Caesar, was a prominent Roman senator and nobleman. (Guillaume Rouillé, from Promptuarii Iconum Insigniorum, *1555)*

Aurelia Cotta, the daughter of the Roman consul Lucius Aurelius Cotta, was the mother of Gaius Julius Caesar. (Guillaume Rouillé, from Promptuarii Iconum Insigniorum, *1555)*

Cornelia Cinnilla was the daughter of Lucius Cornelius Cinna and the first wife of Gaius Julius Caesar. When she was only 11 or 12, she is believed to have become the mother of his daughter Julia Caesaris. Cornelia died in childbirth 15 years later at the age of 26. (Guillaume Rouillé, from Promptuarii Iconum Insigniorum, *1555)*

Julia Caesaris was the daughter of Gaius Julius Caesar, the conqueror, and his only legitimate child. She married her father's co-triumvir Gnaeus Pompeius Magnus in 59 BC, but died in childbirth five years later. (Guillaume Rouillé, from Promptuarii Iconum Insigniorum, *1555)*

Pompeia, the daughter of Quintus Pompeius Rufus, was Julius Caesar's second wife. They were married in 67 BC, but divorced five years later. (Guillaume Rouillé, from Promptuarii Iconum Insigniorum, *1555)*

Calpurnia Pisonis, the daughter of Lucius Calpurnius Piso, was Julius Caesar's third wife, marrying him in 59 BC at the age of 16. They remained married until his death in 44 BC. She never remarried. (Guillaume Rouillé, from Promptuarii Iconum Insigniorum, *1555)*

In the late summer of 55 BC, Julius Caesar became the first Roman general to lead a cross-channel invasion of Britannia. He and his legions were met on the beaches by British cavalry, but nevertheless managed to establish a beachhead. (Author's collection)

An artist's conception of a pair of Gallic warriors, circa the first century BC. In their chronicles, Roman authors made note of their long hair and beards. (Author's collection)

The great Arverni warlord Vercingetorix (left) was the first Gallic leader to unite tribal armies from throughout Gaul to fight the Romans. When he and his great army lost to the Romans at Alesia in 52 BC, he rode to Caesur's camp on his great warhorse and personally offered his surrender. Caesar (right) had him chained and thrown into a prison in Rome. (Author's collection)

Traveling to Alexandria in pursuit of Pompey in 48 BC, Julius Caesar had the opportunity to pay his respects at the mausoleum of his own hero and role model, Alexander the Great. (Author's collection)

When he crossed the Rubicon River with his legions in 49 BC, Julius Caesar defied the established order of the Roman Republic that forbade generals from leading troops into Rome. In so doing, Caesar gambled his reputation and his future on an inevitable civil war—and won. (Author's collection)

In 47 BC, a large number of Roman troops mutinied, demanding payment of promised bonuses. Julius Caesar addressed the mob personally, empathizing with their demands, and soon winning them over with his oratorical skills. When he called them "citizens" rather than "soldiers," they begged to be considered soldiers once again, and to accompany him on his next campaign. (Author's collection)

In 46 BC, Julius Caesar was feted in Rome with a series of four Triumphs celebrating his heroic conquests. The triumphal procession pictured here celebrates Caesar's victory over the Pontic King Pharnaces, whom Caesar defeated so quickly that he was moved to quip "Veni, vidi, Vici" (I came, I saw, I conquered). This image was created around 1598 or 1599 by Andrea Andreani, after the painting by Andrea Mantegna. (Library of Congress Prints and Photographs Division)

Gaius Julius Caesar returned to Rome in 45 BC, having vanquished all his military rivals, and was named Dictator in Perpetuity of the Roman Republic. A year later, his political rivals ended his life, only to see him posthumously deified. (Author's collection)

CHAPTER 14

Vercingetorix, the Ultimate Gallic Warlord

JULIUS CAESAR HAD GONE BACK TO ITALY AT THE END OF THE 53 BC campaigning season confident that he had subdued the unrest that had erupted a year earlier in Gaul. Indeed, in *Commentarii de Bello Gallico* he had the temerity to again use the word *tranquil* to describe Gaul, as he had in 57 BC. However, if 53 BC should have taught him a single lesson, it was how fragile Roman rule in Gaul was.

Perhaps that is why in 53 BC he turned from defeating armies to decimating infrastructure and driving people to the brink of starvation. Perhaps he had decided that this was the only way to subjugate the Gallic people.

A subtle warning that Caesar observed in Gaul was the changing tactics of his enemies. The Gauls had been more successful in battle, handing major defeats to the Romans. The humiliating deaths of Sabinus and Cotta had seriously stung Roman morale. Previously, the Gauls had used hit-and-run tactics, rarely venturing into major fixed battles against the Romans. Now the Gauls were showing increasing willingness to initiate and engage in protracted battles.

These so-called barbarians also had shown a willingness to learn new methods and to use them effectively—the Gauls had deliberately acquired advanced engineering techniques from captured Roman teachers, as in the besieging of Quintus Cicero.

Finally, the rise of Ambiorix, and Caesar's obsession with finding him, make plain the Gauls' interest in having a coalition under a single commander. Things were changing in the Gallic art of war, and Caesar had to have seen it coming.

52 BC began like 53 BC, with serious and unexpected trouble in Gaul. This time Caesar faced the most serious challenge of his Gallic Wars, and that which he had feared most—a coalition of enemy tribes unified under a charismatic and tactically perceptive commander.

The man was Vercingetorix, a leader who emerged from among the nobility of the Arverni people, who lived in the mountainous country that is now the Auvergne Region of southeastern France. He was the son of an ambitious warlord named Celtillus, who had been killed by fellow Gauls while trying to unify all Gaul under his own rule. His son harbored similar ambitions, making him an appropriate rival to Caesar.

Vercingetorix's hometown was Gergovia, the city described by the first-century Greek geographer Strabo as the "metropolis of the Arverni." It is now part of the French town of La Roche-Blanche, but in 52 BC it was an Arverni city; Caesar had resettled some of the Boii people nearby after defeating them in his war against the Helvetii in 58 BC.

Vercingetorix had been consolidating his power since well before the 52 BC campaigning season. As Caesar describes it in *Commentarii de Bello Gallico,* "Having collected such a body of troops, he brings over to his sentiments such of his fellow-citizens as he has access to; he exhorts them to take up arms in behalf of the general freedom, and having assembled great forces he drives from the state his opponents, by whom he had been expelled a short time previously. He is saluted king by his partisans; he sends ambassadors in every direction, he conjures them to adhere firmly to their promise."

Caesar goes on to note that Vercingetorix almost immediately enlisted the support of other tribes, specifically naming the Aulerci, Cadurci, Lemovice, Parisii, Pictones, Senones, Turones, and "all the others who border on the ocean." The last presumably included the Veneti, whom Caesar had spent so much time bringing to heel. Caesar adds, "The supreme command is conferred on [Vercingetorix] by unanimous consent" of the tribes.

The speed at which the tribes unanimously consented suggests there was a great pent-up demand for a single leader, and a universal recognition that the time was right to challenge the Romans. Even as Caesar was still wintering in Italy, Vercingetorix had succeeded beyond what Ambiorix or any other Gallic leader had managed to achieve in this regard.

When the stunning news of the coalition came, Caesar was pre-occupied at home by political turmoil, but he had no choice. He had to return to Gaul without waiting for spring. Immediate action was required not only to counter Vercingetorix but to demonstrate to the other tribes across Gaul that the Romans were on top of things and this was not an auspicious time for other rebellions.

Caesar had not yet reached Transalpine Gaul when Vercingetorix and his coalition partners began marching against the tribes that had remained loyal to the Romans. Vercingetorix dispatched Lucterius, a leader of the Cadurci, to attack the Ruteni, while Vercingetorix himself led his army of Arverni against the Bituriges, whose major cities were Avaricum and Noviodunum Biturigum, located near the present French cities of Bourges and Neungsur-Beuvron, respectively.

The Bituriges were under the protection of the Aedui, who lived across the Loire River from them, and who had been among Caesar's most reliable allies since he first arrived in Gaul six years earlier. With Vercingetorix preparing to attack them, the Bituriges sent a request for assistance to the Aedui. However, even as they were coming to the aid of the Bituriges, the Aedui suspected treachery on the part of their clients. Fearing that their friends were about to switch sides, and that they were engineering a trap, the Aedui stopped short of crossing the river. Whether it would have happened otherwise is not certain, but the Bituriges immediately joined the Vercingetorix coalition.

When Caesar finally reached Transalpine Gaul, Lucterius had already defeated the Nitiobriges and Gabali, as well as the Ruteni, and was starting his march against the great Roman center on the Mediterranean coast at Narbo. Caesar decided that his first priority should be to head off the enemy there. When he saw the Romans marching against him in force, Lucterius backed off and decided not to penetrate an area that was well defended by Roman garrisons.

Caesar then marched north to intercept Lucterius, crossing into the Cévennes mountains, where the late winter snow still lay six feet deep in the passes. The Arverni, who were besieging the Boii in Gergovia, assumed that the Romans would never get across the Cévennes at that time of year, but they were wrong. Nobody was more surprised than Vercingetorix to learn from messengers that Caesar was approaching.

However, Caesar needed to deal with two immediate concerns before he attacked Vercingetorix head-on. He needed to marshal his wintering legions into an army, and he needed to stop the attacks by Vercingetorix's allies against tribes that were still Roman allies, especially the Aedui. Vercingetorix was threatening the Aedui and their client tribes because, as Caesar interprets, "all Gaul should revolt when the tributaries of the Aedui were subdued, because it would appear that there was in [Caesar] no protection for his friends." In other words, Caesar had to support the Aedui now if he wanted to expect their support in the campaign against Vercingetorix.

To address these issues Caesar went deep into north-central Gaul, through the territory of the Aedui into that of the Lingone, and to Agendicum, where some of the legions had been in winter quarters. He established a base camp and supply dump at Agendicum, and he left what he describes as "the luggage of the entire army" there so that the legions could move more quickly.

For the 52 BC spring campaign Caesar writes that he marched with a total of ten legions, with Titus Labienus as his second in command, plus a sizable cavalry contingent that included Aeduan horsemen. He also mentions that he surrounded himself with a contingent of 400 handpicked Germanic cavalrymen.

The next move for Caesar's army was to attack the fortified garrison cities of Vercingetorix's allies in north-central Gaul before heading south toward Vercingetorix and Gergovia.

Caesar sent Gaius Trebonius to besiege Vellaunodunum, and Caesar himself led two legions against Cenabum (now Orléans) on the Loire. When the inhabitants attempted to flee under cover of darkness, Caesar attacked, taking "possession of the town so completely, that very few of the whole number of the enemy escaped being taken alive, because the narrowness of the bridge and the roads prevented the multitude from escaping."

Caesar marched onward, besieging the stronghold at Noviodunum Biturigum, whose name literally means "Hill Fort of the Bituriges." Hearing of this, Vercingetorix broke off his siege of Gergovia and marched north to meet Caesar.

Meanwhile, the people of Noviodunum Biturigum capitulated, begging Caesar to accept their surrender and spare their lives. As the Romans were collecting captured arms and horses, and processing hostages, the cavalry vanguard of Vercingetorix's army showed up on the crest of a nearby hill. Seeing this, the leaders in Noviodunum Biturigum retracted their surrender and ordered that people take up arms against the Romans. Caesar quickly ordered his men out of the city to face the more serious threat from the Arverni army.

Caesar's horsemen soundly defeated the Arverni in a cavalry battle, with the survivors retreating to the main body of Vercingetorix's army.

Caesar then turned his attention back to Noviodunum Biturigum, where once again the Bituriges begged for his mercy, handing over those who had reneged on the previous surrender. When he had wrapped up the situation there, Caesar resumed his march, setting his sights on Avaricum, the other key city of the Bituriges, which he describes as the tribe's "largest and best fortified town."

Contemplating the nonstop string of successes by the Romans in quickly taking every city in their path, Vercingetorix now decided on a desperate change of strategy. The Roman legions were moving quickly because they carried minimal supplies, obtaining food locally as they marched. In order to counter this, Vercingetorix ordered a scorched earth policy, so that, as Caesar writes, "the Romans should be prevented from foraging and procuring provisions." Essentially, Vercingetorix would destroy the towns himself to keep them from being captured by the Romans.

The cavalry of the Arverni was literally scorching the earth, having been ordered to burn houses and stockpiles of food throughout the land. Caesar mentions that more than 20 towns of the Bituriges were burned in one day.

Vercingetorix and his commanders even debated whether Avaricum itself should be burned or defended. The Bituriges begged Vercingetorix not to "be compelled to set fire with their own hands to the fairest city of almost the whole of Gaul, which was both a protection and ornament to the state." They promised to defend it against the Romans, and Vercingetorix relented, stationing a garrison of Arverni there. He then established his own main camp outside the city.

Caesar soon arrived and set about besieging Avaricum, approaching it with siege towers. However, when he learned that Vercingetorix was on the outside, and preparing for a surprise attack, Caesar ordered his men to prepare for a field battle.

Vercingetorix held the high ground, a gently sloping hill separated from the Roman position by a broad swamp. Arverni troops guarded every ford. Caesar therefore decided not to be drawn into a battle with Vercingetorix but to persist with the siege of the city. His legionaries grumbled about his ducking a fight, but they were on short rations and the city contained food.

In turn, Vercingetorix's troops complained when he did not attack Caesar. To this he replied that the Romans were going to starve before they took Avaricum by siege, and they would be defeated without any losses of Arverni troops.

In an impressive feat of engineering the Romans built two giant parallel earthworks on which the siege towers would be rolled perpendicular to the city wall. They also built a wall to allow troops to move back and forth between these two terraces.

For more than three weeks the Bituriges defended their town well, attacking the Romans as they worked, burning the wooden structures that the Romans built to protect themselves from spears and arrows, and mining tunnels beneath the earthworks to collapse them. The Bituriges spilled boiling oil on legionaries who approached too closely and built towers to match the height of the Roman siege towers. In their defense against the Romans, the Bituriges had an ally in the cold, rainy weather.

In the meantime Vercingetorix continued harassing attacks against the Romans, but they failed to dissuade the Romans from the single-minded task of building their siege machinery.

As the Romans showed no sign of slacking off, the soldiers of the Bituriges inside the city grew worried and considered sneaking out of the city—much to the consternation of their women and children, who would be left behind by the troops, as they would slow down their retreat.

The elaborate Roman siege mechanism was finally completed after 25 days, just as the morale of the Bituriges collapsed. Caesar then ordered his legionaries "to reap, at least, the harvest of victory proportionate to their exertions [offering] a reward for those who should first scale the walls, and gave the signal to the soldiers."

In *Commentarii de Bello Gallico* Caesar goes on to explain,

The enemy being alarmed by the suddenness of the attack, were dislodged from the wall and towers, and drew up, in form of a wedge, in the market place and the open streets, with this intention that, if an attack should be made on any side, they should fight with their line drawn up to receive it. When they saw no one descending to the level ground, and the enemy extending themselves along the entire wall in every direction, fearing lest every hope of flight should be cut off, they cast away their arms, and sought, without stopping, the most remote parts of the town.

The Romans crested the walls, opened the gates, and flooded into the city. Because of "the fatigue of the siege, they spared neither those worn out with years, women, nor children. Finally, out of all that number, which amounted to about 40,000, scarcely 800, who fled from the town when they heard the first alarm, reached Vercingetorix in safety."

Vercingetorix blamed the Bituriges for their own defeat and withdrew his army toward Gergovia, which the Arverni had captured during the prolonged siege of Avaricum.

In the wake of the massacre the hungry Romans feasted on captured food and enjoyed a well-deserved rest. It had already been a busy year for Julius Caesar, and it was only June. He now divided his forces for the next phase of the campaign. He ordered Labienus to take four legions and head north again into the area of the headwaters of the Seine River, south of the present city of Paris. Caesar himself would take six legions and travel south, continuing the long march to Gergovia. The auxiliary cavalry was divided between these two contingents, with Caesar taking a 10,000-man contingent of Aeduan troops commanded by an officer named Litaviccus.

The march to Gergovia took the Romans through the valley of the Allier River, a tributary of the Loire. The river was bridged at a number of places along the route, but Vercingetorix had destroyed these bridges. This made Caesar's progress more challenging as the river was in its high-water stage, and fording it was difficult.

Vercingetorix reached Gergovia well ahead of Caesar, so the Arverni had time to prepare for the expected Roman siege. The Arverni were in good shape to do battle. Although Caesar had an unbroken series of siege victories, and Vercingetorix had failed to stop him, the Gallic coalition held. Indeed, it was actually strengthened when Teutomarus of the Nitiobriges, who had also been loyal friends of the Romans, joined Vercingetorix.

As Caesar arrived at Gergovia, five days after getting his legions across the Allier, he found that Vercingetorix had "pitched his camp on the mountain near the town, placed the forces of each state separately and at small intervals around himself. [He had] occupied all the hills of that range as far as they commanded a view [of the Roman positions], he presented a formidable appearance."

Cavalry skirmishing began right away and continued for the next few days as the two commanders sized up their respective positions. Caesar made the first move, capturing a mountain near the main plateau where Gergovia was, and he stationed two legions to hold this high ground. Still, the main plateau constituted an ideal defensive position from which Vercingetorix could hold off any frontal attack. Caesar would have to besiege the place.

Vercingetorix made the next move, bribing the Aeduan leader Convictolitavis to convince Litaviccus to switch sides and attack the Romans. When Caesar learned of this defection, he mobilized four legions to attack the Aedui. Although Litaviccus escaped to Gergovia,

Caesar was able to convince the majority of the Aedui to remain loyal. However, back in the Aeduan homeland, Convictolitavis was able to foment a rebellion against the Romans. He roused anger at the pressure on the Aedui to increase supplies from their own stockpiles to feed the Romans after the earlier scorched earth policy among the Bituriges had wiped out the only other available food source. The revolt of the Aedui left Caesar with a dilemma. Should he move now to put down the insurrection or proceed with the siege of Gergovia?

He chose the latter, although he recognized that he also needed to address the problem of the Aedui in a timely manner. He had originally hoped to execute a protracted siege, essentially starving the Arverni into submission, but this would take more time than he now had.

After he captured some outlying Gallic positions, Caesar crafted a ruse to lure his enemy into a decisive battle in the open. The idea was to feign a tactical withdrawal as bait to get Vercingetorix out of Gergovia.

With his legions close to the Gergovia walls, Caesar ordered the trumpets to signal a retreat. The men of Legio X, whom Caesar himself accompanied, heard the signal, but others did not. Instead of withdrawing, as they should have done had they heard the signal, they attacked. When they got over the walls, Gergovia seemed to lay ripe for plucking.

Caesar colorfully describes in *Commentarii de Bello Gallico* the chaotic rush on Gergovia: "Lucius Fabius a centurion of Legio VIII, who, it was ascertained, had said that day among his fellow soldiers that he was excited by the plunder of Avaricum, and would not allow any one to mount the wall before him, finding three men of his own company, and being raised up by them, scaled the wall. He himself, in turn, taking hold of them one by one drew them up to the wall."

From his vantage point Caesar could see that the uncoordinated assault on the wall was tactically unsound, but his only choice now was to send more troops in to try to stabilize the position. As he writes, "The fight was going on most vigorously, hand to hand, and the enemy depended on their position and numbers, our men on their bravery. . . . Lucius Fabius the centurion, and those who had scaled the wall with him, being surrounded and slain, were cast from the wall. Marcus Petreius, a centurion of the same legion, after attempting to hew down the gates, was overpowered by numbers. . . . Thus he fell fighting a few moments after, and saved his men by his own death."

Caesar goes on to say:

Our soldiers, being hard pressed on every side, were dislodged from their position, with the loss of 46 centurions; but Legio X, which had been posted in reserve on ground a little more level, checked the Gauls in their eager pursuit. It was supported by the cohorts of Legio XIII, which, being led from the smaller camp, had, under the command of Titus Sextius, occupied the higher ground. The legions, as soon as they reached the plain, halted and faced the enemy. Vercingetorix led back his men from the part of the hill within the fortifications. On that day little less than 700 of the [Roman] soldiers were missing.

The following day Caesar

censured the rashness and avarice of [the Roman] soldiers, in that they had judged for themselves how far they ought to proceed, or what they ought to do, and could not be kept back by the tribunes of the soldiers and the lieutenants. . . . As much as [I] admired the greatness of their courage, since neither the fortifications of the camp, nor the height of the mountain, nor the wall of the town could retard them; in the same degree he censured their licentiousness and arrogance, because they thought that they knew more than their general concerning victory, and the issue of actions and that he required in his soldiers forbearance and self-command, no less than valor and magnanimity.

Vercingetorix recognized that Roman "rashness and avarice" had handed him a victory, and he kept the bulk of his Gallic coalition army in place, behind the walls high on the plateau, sending only a small cavalry contingent down to harass the Romans. He would not be lured out now.

The following day, when Caesar led his six legions back down the Allier "in the direction of the Aedui," he was withdrawing for real—easily interpreted by the Gauls as a retreat—leaving Vercingetorix in control of Gergovia.

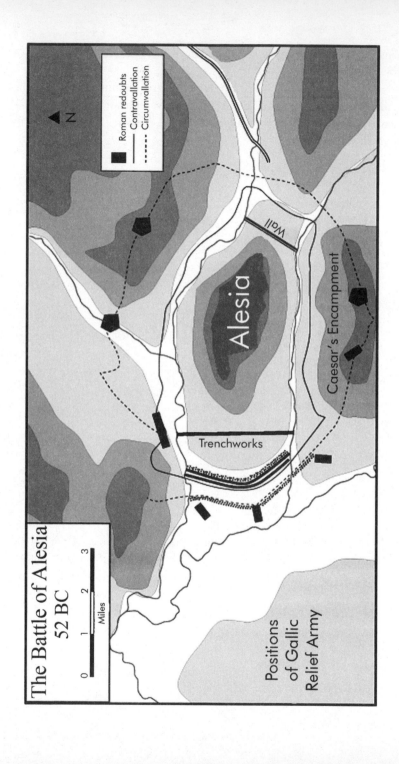

CHAPTER 15

The Battle of Alesia
52 BC

0   1   2   3
Miles

N

Roman redoubts
Contravallation
Circumvallation

Alesia

Wall

Caesar's Encampment

Trenchworks

Positions
of Gallic
Relief Army

The Battle of Alesia

As Julius Caesar led his legions away from Gergovia in the early summer of 52 BC, his disappointment at not having had a decisive battle against Vercingetorix perhaps was matched only by Vercingetorix's disappointment at not having had the chance to defeat the Roman general once and for all.

Both men understood that a Gallic victory, particularly one in which Caesar was killed or captured, could touch off an irreversible unraveling of Roman rule throughout Gaul. Likewise, if the rebellion among the Aedui, till now Rome's most crucial Gallic allies, were to spread, no Roman leader except Caesar himself would be able to stop it.

For Caesar the problem was like that in Belgica in 54–53 BC but worse. The Aedui were setting an example for Rome's friends and foes alike: it was time to rebel and join the undefeated Vercingetorix with his great coalition of tribes.

As Caesar marched north, he received a bit of good news. Titus Labienus had marched from Agendicum to crush the insurgency of the Senones and to defeat the Parisii at Lutetia (now the city of Paris). Once the two Romans linked up, they had an army of 12 legions to address the Aeduan insurgency.

It was not a moment too soon. Things were spiraling out of control. As Caesar writes, "The revolt of the Aedui being known, the war grows more dangerous. Embassies are sent by them in all directions: as far as they can prevail by influence, authority, or money, they strive to excite the state[s to rebel against the Romans]....A council of all Gaul is summoned to [the Aeduan capital at] Bibracte. They come together in great numbers and from every quarter to the same place. The decision is left to the votes of the mass: all to a man approve of Vercingetorix as their general."

Inspired by the apparent defeat of Caesar at Gergovia, the Gallic coalition army was growing rapidly. Efforts were even made to lure the Helvetii in the Alps, as well as the Allobroges of Transalpine Gaul, into the coalition. Only three tribes north of Transalpine Gaul were absent from this summit conference, the Remi and Lingones, because they remained loyal to Caesar, and the Treviri because they were preoccupied with cross-Rhine raids by Germani.

Aware that Caesar planned to attack, Vercingetorix, who had left Gergovia, prepared a defensive position with, according to Caesar's estimate, 80,000 troops. This was roughly equal in number to Caesar's 12 legions plus their auxiliaries. The site was a hilltop citadel, giving the Gallic army a high-ground advantage similar to that at Gergovia; the location was called Alesia, somewhere in eastern France, about 150 miles northeast of Gergovia.

The exact location has been the subject of speculation, but by the end of the twentieth century, archeological investigations had narrowed the list of potential sites considerably. These include Alaise in the Franche-comte Region and Chaux-des-Crotenay near the Jura mountains. Most historians support the theory that Alesia was Mont Auxois near the French town of Alise-Sainte-Reine, about 30 miles northwest of Dijon.

Caesar marched to a place overlooking Alesia in late August 52 BC and began to contemplate his next move. In *Commentarii de Bello Gallico* he describes the city as being "situated on the top of a hill, in a very lofty position, so that it did not appear likely to be taken, except by a regular siege. Two rivers, on two different sides, washed the foot of the hill. Before the town lay a plain of about three miles in length; on every other side hills at a moderate distance, and of an equal degree of height, surrounded the town."

Because Vercingetorix had chosen a defensive position reminiscent of Gergovia, Caesar revisited his original plan for the siege of Gergovia—what he would have done if he'd had the time. He would surround the place and starve the Gauls out.

He ordered his engineers to encircle the 11-mile circumference of the hill with a circumvallation of 15-foot trenches and 13-foot-high wooden fortifications. This line was punctuated by 23 redoubts from which observers could spot any movements by the Gauls against the line.

The massive undertaking was completed in just three weeks, during which time the Gauls initiated numerous cavalry skirmishes to harass the construction crews, and at least one major Gallic assault against a segment of the circumvallation. As Caesar writes, "[A] great slaughter ensues; some leave their horses, and endeavor to cross the ditch and climb the wall.... Vercingetorix orders the gates to be shut, lest the camp should be left undefended." Caesar's elite Germanic cavalry chased the enemy back to its hill fort, whereupon the riders "retreated, after slaying many and taking several horses."

Around this time Vercingetorix must have started to appreciate the mistake in remaining in his defensive position, waiting and watching while the Romans fortified their own lines. The better choice would have been to attack and force a great field battle when Caesar had only just arrived.

Vercingetorix realized that he was about to be surrounded and that he was down to 30 days' rations, so he decided to send for reinforcements. In the dark of night Gallic horsemen slipped through the unfinished line. Caesar writes that Vercingetorix had ordered each man to "go to his respective state, and press for the war all who were old enough to bear arms."

At this point Caesar ordered construction of a 14-mile outside line that pointed outward, called a contravallation. The Roman troops were now inside the doughnut-shaped area between these two concentric fortified lines.

As Caesar himself describes it, the contravallation involved trench-works 20 feet deep, with vertical sides. As seen on the map accompanying this chapter, these encompassed so extensive an area that the whole defensive works could not easily be surrounded by a line of soldiers. Caesar ordered several additional trenches dug across access points to the enemy compound, including two that were 15 feet wide by 15 feet deep and filled with water channeled from the nearby river. Behind these the Romans built a wall that was 12 feet high, with large stakes to prevent the enemy from scaling it. They also erected as many as two dozen guard towers at intervals of about 80 feet.

In fact, as thorough as the Roman engineers were, neither the 11 miles of the inner circumvallation nor the 14 miles of the outer contravallation were solid, uninterrupted lines. There were places—Caesar notes a hill on the north side—where natural anomalies in the terrain made it impossible to build all the specified details of the works.

The battle plan called for cavalry to be posted in groups throughout the doughnut-shaped inner line and shifted to wherever they were needed to meet a specific attack. Caesar notes that his lieutenants Gaius Trebonius and Mark Antony were in command of this operation.

Meanwhile, the Gallic leaders who had been asked for reinforcements pondered what to do about providing relief at Alesia. According to Caesar, they decided that "all who could bear arms should not be called out, which was the opinion of Vercingetorix, but that a fixed number should be levied from each state; lest, when so great a multitude assembled together, they could neither govern nor distinguish their men, nor have the means of supplying them with corn."

By Caesar's estimate the total size of the Gallic army coming to relieve Vercingetorix at Alesia, and to annihilate Caesar and the Romans, exceeded a quarter of a million men. His summary states that there were 8,000 cavalry, and about 240,000 infantry. He notes that the largest contingents were 35,000 from the Aedui and their associated dependencies; another 35,000 from the Arverni, Eleuteti, Cadurci, Gabali, and Velauni; as well as 30,000 from the Rauraci and the Boii (of whom Caesar had been overly considerate in the past).

Caesar mentions that the source of the numbers was a calculation made by the supreme commanders of the enemy army, including Vergasillaunus of the Arverni, a cousin of Vercingetorix's. Whether Caesar exaggerated the numbers is not known but probable. By how much will never be known.

The essential facts were that a massive outpouring of Gallic manpower was flowing toward Alesia in late September 52 BC (as described in the introduction), and that when these troops arrived, the Romans would be vastly outnumbered. This huge effort demonstrated a desire for a showdown and underscored the great power of Vercingetorix as a rallying point for pan-Gallic resistance to Roman rule.

Caesar candidly spoke of his former allies among the Gauls and how their friendship no longer mattered to him. He writes that "such was the unanimity of the Gauls in asserting their freedom, and recovering their ancient renown in war, that they were influenced neither by favors, nor by the recollection of private friendship; and all earnestly directed their energies and resources to that war."

Inside Alesia, meanwhile, Vercingetorix had no idea whether or when a relief army would be coming, and he certainly had no idea of the immense size. As Caesar writes, "Those who were blockaded at Alesia, the day being past on which they had expected auxiliaries from their countrymen, and all their corn being consumed, ignorant of what was going on among the Aedui, convened an assembly and deliberated on the exigency of their situation.... Various opinions had been expressed among them, some of which proposed a surrender, others a sally, whilst their strength would support it."

In *Commentarii de Bello Gallico* Caesar quotes a speech given inside Alesia by an Arverni nobleman who decried the notion of giving up, saying in part:

> I shall pay no attention to the opinion of those who call a most disgraceful surrender by the name of a capitulation; nor do I think that they ought to be considered as citizens, or summoned to the council. My business is with those who approve of a sally: in whose advice the memory of our ancient prowess seems to dwell in the opinion of you all. To be unable to bear privation for a short time is disgraceful cowardice, not

true valor.... Do you suppose that the Romans are employed every day in the outer fortifications for mere amusement? But what other motive or wish have the Romans, than, induced by envy, to settle in the lands and states of those whom they have learned by fame to be noble and powerful in war, and impose on them perpetual slavery? For they never have carried on wars on any other terms.

As rations ran out, the Mandubii, whose town Alesia was, attempted to surrender their wives and children, begging the Romans to "receive them as slaves and relieve them with food." However, Caesar placed guards on the ramparts and "forbade them to be admitted."

The following day the reinforcements started showing up, camping on hilltops overlooking the Roman positions. Excitement swept through the besieged Alesia. Cavalry skirmishing began, and Gallic archers peppered the Romans with arrows. Caesar's own Germanic cavalry "made a charge against the enemy [Gallic horsemen] in a compact body, and drove them back; and, when they were put to flight, the archers were surrounded and cut to pieces."

The main attack began at midnight on September 30–October 1 (by the pre-Julian calendar of the Roman Republic), with the Gallic infantry silently approaching the contravallation with scaling ladders and metal hooks to storm the Roman ramparts.

When they struck the contravallation, Vercingetorix ordered a simultaneous attack against the circumvallation. However, in the dark the Gauls became impaled on the spikes that studded the Roman defenses, creating confusion and splintering unit cohesion.

Wherever they seemed to threaten the Roman line, they were met by a concentration of defenders. Antony and Trebonius masterfully managed their cavalry assets, moving them quickly to points on the line where they were needed to hold off an attack, then moving them quickly elsewhere.

The night assaults against the Roman lines failed miserably. Caesar writes that the Gauls were "twice repulsed with great loss," indicating that they made two major efforts to achieve a breakthrough against the Romans.

After scouting the Roman lines for weaknesses, notably the hill on the north side, the commanders of the Gallic relief force formulated a plan. Vergasillaunus would lead a concentrated assault with a 60,000-man force on October 2. Vercingetorix, who was watching the actions of the relief force so that he could act in concert when it made a move, launched a coordinated attack. Caesar writes that the enemy struck "on all sides at once...they flocked to whatever part of the works seemed weakest."

Caesar goes on to say that the Romans met the enemy in every assault. Caesar himself, having selected a position where he could see most of the line, ordered his troops about, matching defense to offense. To his dismay he saw that the Gauls had moved in piles of dirt to bridge a section of the line. Describing the situation and the exhaustion of his men, Caesar writes, "Our men have no longer arms or strength."

To respond to this crisis he sent Labienus with six cohorts to relieve the overwhelmed legionaries, but Gauls were already inside Roman lines. They were filling in the ditches and tearing down ramparts and breastworks with hooks and ropes.

Fearing a general collapse of the Roman lines, Caesar brought his most heroic oratory skills to bear. According to *Commentarii de Bello Gallico,* he exhorted the legionaries "not to succumb to the toil...the fruits of all former engagements depend on [this] day and hour."

He flooded the breach in the line with an additional 13 cohorts, and personally led a mixed infantry and cavalry contingent to make a circuit of the external fortifications in the hope of outflanking Vergasillaunus. Amazingly, this brash move worked, and suddenly Caesar and his fearless cavalrymen were in the Gallic rear. When the cohorts on the line saw this, they rapidly went from defense to offense.

As Caesar writes, "The enemy turn their backs; the cavalry intercept them in their flight, and a great slaughter ensues. Sedulius the general and chief of the Lemovices is slain; Vergasillaunus, the Arvernian, is taken alive in the flight."

Caesar notes that 74 military standards were brought to him, indicating that 74 enemy units were defeated. He adds, "Few out of so great a number return safe to their camp. The besieged, beholding from the town the slaughter and flight of their countrymen, despairing of safety, lead back their troops from the fortifications."

The news of the rout of 60,000 caused an overall panic among the remaining Gallic armies, and they stumbled over one another to retreat as fast as they could. Seeing this, the Romans gave chase. Caesar writes that had the legionaries "not been wearied by sending frequent reinforcements, and the labor of the entire day, all the enemy's forces could have been destroyed."

Shortly after midnight he sent his cavalry to relieve the pursuing infantry and overtake the rear of the Gallic retreat, observing that "a great number are taken or cut to pieces, the rest by flight escape in different directions to their respective states."

Caesar offers his own explanation of the abrupt collapse of the Gallic armies in a memorable line from *Commentarii de Bello Gallico:* "For as the temper of the Gauls is impetuous and ready to undertake wars, so their mind is weak, and by no means resolute in enduring calamities."

On October 3 Caesar received a message about Vercingetorix, sent out from the hopelessly surrounded Alesia garrison. The Gauls asked whether they "should wish to atone to the Romans by his death, or surrender him alive."

Caesar responded by ordering "their arms to be surrendered, and their chieftains delivered up." He then seated himself at the head of the lines in front of the camp as the Gallic chieftains, including Vercingetorix himself, were brought before him.

Plutarch offers a much more colorful description of this momentous surrender, writing that "the leader of the whole war, Vercingetorix, after putting on his most beautiful armor and decorating his horse, rode out through the gate. He made a circuit around Caesar, who remained seated, and then leaped down from his horse, stripped off his suit of armor, and seating himself at Caesar's feet, remained motionless, until he was delivered up to be kept in custody for the Triumph."

Indeed, Vercingetorix was taken to Rome in chains, where he languished in a cell. After he was exhibited in the Triumph held in Caesar's honor in 46 BC, Vercingetorix was executed.

Like Ambiorix among the Belgians, Vercingetorix emerged as a nationalistic folk hero among the French. In 1865 the emperor Napoleon III commissioned a 23-foot heroic statue of Vercingetorix to be erected on the supposed site of Alesia at Alise-Sainte-Reine. On the base an inscription composed by the great architect and essayist Eugène Emmanuel Violletle-Duc reads, "Gaul united, Forming a single nation, Animated by a common spirit, Can defy the Universe."

Gaul and its favorite son had not, however, been able to defy Julius Caesar.

If Gergovia marked a low point in the military career of Julius Caesar thus far, the Battle of Alesia was his greatest triumph. Caesar's victory there marked the end of the Gallic Wars. After that day in 52 BC, there were no further threats to Caesar or to Roman rule within Gaul.

CHAPTER 16

Crossing the Rubicon into Civil War

DURING THE GALLIC WARS, JULIUS CAESAR, HAD BECOME AN ENOR-
mously popular national idol. With his exploits in Britannia and
Germania and his long string of victories, culminating with Alesia,
he was probably the greatest hero in Roman history to date. He
was easily the most powerful and well-loved Roman leader outside
Rome.

He had also grown wealthy during his conquests, and he used his
fortune to remake himself as a popular philanthropist. As Suetonius
writes, "He took no less pains to win the devotion of princes and
provinces all over the world, offering prisoners to some by the thousand as a gift, and sending auxiliary troops to the aid of others when-
ever they wished, and as often as they wished, without the sanction
of the senate or people, besides adorning the principal cities of Asia
and Greece with magnificent public works, as well as those of Italy
and the provinces of Gaul and Hispania."

Inside Rome, as Caesar was scoring his seven-year string of victories, his fellow triumvirs Marcus Licinius Crassus and Gnaeus Pompeius Magnus squabbled, making themselves appear petty in comparison with Caesar. Being out of town had the advantage of keeping Caesar apart from the political machinations of the capital.

Like Caesar, Crassus and Pompey had also been given proconsulships—Crassus in Syria, and Pompey in both provinces of Hispania. But despite their skill in the trenches of domestic politics, neither had the competence or acumen to do with their domains what Caesar had done in Gaul. Crassus tried to emulate the successful conquests of Caesar but was killed in 53 BC in the Battle of Carrhae while leading a failed invasion of Parthia. By this time the Parthians had defeated and absorbed the Seleucid Empire, a remnant of Alexander the Great's empire, and ruled a vast swath of territory from Turkey to the Indus River, encompassing what is now Iraq, Iran, Afghanistan, and Pakistan. For the ambitious Crassus to defeat them would have been an accomplishment to rival Caesar's in Gaul. In the battle Crassus panicked and sacrificed mobility for a more defensive formation, which collapsed and was annihilated in a defeat embarrassing to the Romans. This served only to make Caesar's victories seem more extraordinary.

With the death of Crassus the triumvirate was no more, and Pompey was now the most powerful man in Rome.

The disaffection between the most powerful man in Rome and the most powerful Roman outside the capital gradually increased. While Pompey was involved in the day-to-day political maneuverings in the capital, Caesar was away in Gaul, above the petty political fray and accomplishing what Rome perceived as great things. Like Crassus, who had gotten himself killed trying to emulate Caesar, Pompey was jealous of the prestige that Caesar had earned, especially because he earned it while so far away that the public saw only the great things. Pompey was visible, warts and all, while Caesar was a heroic portrait. Relations between Pompey and Caesar were certainly soured when Pompey's wife, who was Caesar's daughter Julia, died in childbirth in 54 BC—and Pompey married Cornelia, the daughter of Caesar's political opponent, the staunch Optimate Quintus Metellus Scipio.

By the time of Caesar's victory at Alesia, Pompey ruled as sole consul. Jealous of Caesar's popularity, accomplishments, and his potential as a rival, Pompey sought to marginalize him by keeping him at a distance, away from active participation in politics. Caesar himself was ready to announce his own plan to run for consul. His proconsulship in Gaul was due to expire in 50 BC, at which time Pompey and the Senate formally ordered Caesar to return to Rome.

However, Roman law prohibited a commander from bringing a military force across the Rubicon River, which marked the boundary between Cisalpine Gaul and Italy, without Senate approval; the reason was to prevent a military coup.

Caesar realized that he could not abide by this law. He did not trust Pompey and was concerned about returning to the capital defenseless. He had no choice. In January 49 BC, Caesar saddled up and marched south with Legio XIII. As Plutarch writes, "As if abandoning calculation and casting himself upon the future, and uttering the phrase with which men usually prelude their plunge into desperate and daring fortunes, 'Let the die be cast,' he hastened to cross the river."

In crossing the Rubicon he broke the law, alarmed Pompey, and took the first step in a bloody conflict that is often called Caesar's Civil War. The political divide that had sprung up between the Populares, who supported Caesar, and the Optimates, who backed Pompey, would soon become a battle line.

Caesar moved quickly, marching unopposed down the east coast of Italy. City after city gave itself over to the great hero without a fight. It was more like a triumphal march than a military campaign.

Pompey decided that Rome could not be defended against its favorite son and fled the capital accompanied by aristocrats and fellow Optimate politicians. They retreated to Brindisium, on the heel of the Italian peninsula opposite Greece. There Pompey was joined by Metellus Scipio and the incorruptible Marcus Porcius Cato (aka Cato the Younger). Cato had long been a leading opponent of the triumvirate in the Senate, and when the triumvirate ended, he found himself on the same side as Pompey in opposition to Caesar, whom Cato deemed a threat to the Roman political establishment.

Though he had two legions, Legio I and Legio XV, under his command, Pompey was unwilling and afraid to face Caesar in battle. Instead, Pompey ordered another member of the Senate, Lucius Domitius Ahenobarbus, to attack Caesar. Operating under the assumption that Pompey meant to bolster him with the two legions after the battle was joined, Ahenobarbus confronted Caesar at Corfinium, due east of Rome, with only about 30 cohorts.

This fight, the only serious effort to halt Caesar's spring 49 BC advance into Italy, was a failure. Pompey never intervened, and the outnumbered Ahenobarbus was compelled by his own men to surrender. These troops were then gladly incorporated into Caesar's own command. Magnanimously spared by Caesar, Ahenobarbus tried and failed to commit suicide and lived to fight another day.

His command now augmented by the addition of Ahenobarbus's men, Caesar continued south for a showdown with Pompey at Brindisium. There he offered to end the war and proposed that he and his former confederate reconcile, agree to resume their alliance, and rule together again.

Pompey haughtily insisted that he, as Rome's sole consul, outranked Caesar and that, by crossing the Rubicon, Caesar had made himself an enemy of the Senate and the people of Rome. Pompey's refusal of Caesar's proposal ensured that their political power struggle would devolve into a serious and bloody civil war.

Before Caesar's engineers could build a causeway to cut off the entrance to the harbor at Brindisium, Pompey assembled a fleet of transport ships and escaped with his legions and fellow politicians across the Adriatic Sea to Epirus, in Roman-colonized Greece. There the consul hoped to assemble an army large enough to defeat Julius Caesar decisively.

Lacking a fleet of his own, Caesar returned to Rome, arriving in mid-March. With Pompey, as well as Scipio and Cato, in exile, Caesar was now the de facto ruler of Rome and its dominions.

Strategically, Pompey was in a strange predicament. To escape Caesar he had gone east to Greece, announcing his intention to raise an army, when far to the west he already had one.

In Hispania, more than 1,500 miles away, were seven legions loyal to Pompey. Five legions in Hispania Citerior (Nearer Hispania) were commanded by the legati Marcus Petreius and Lucius Afranius, while two in Hispania Ulterior (Further Hispania) were commanded by Marcus Varro. Although each legion loyal to Pompey had a commander, the superior command structure to meld them into an army was absent because Pompey was far to the east in Greece.

Caesar embarked from Rome almost immediately to attack these legions before they could move against him on Pompey's behalf. Caesar clearly recognized the irony of the situation. According to Suetonius, Caesar announced, "I go to meet an army without a leader, and I shall return to meet a leader [Pompey] without an army."

The route to Hispania took Caesar first to Massilia (now Marseille, France), which he besieged in advance of the arrival of Ahenobarbus, whom Pompey had sent to reinforce the city. Caesar left his able lieutenant Gaius Trebonius to handle the siege of Massilia and continued to Hispania, a march he completed in only 27 days. By the time Caesar arrived, he had been joined by additional troops, bringing the total strength of his army to six legions, plus 3,000 cavalry.

Caesar had taken control of the passes through the Pyrenees and continued about 100 miles into Hispania Citerior. There, in June 49 BC, he confronted the Pompeian legions commanded by Afranius and Petreius. They were camped on a hill near the city of Ilerda (now Lleida, Spain) on the west side of the rain-swollen Sicoris River (now the Segre). After repairing flood-damaged bridges, Caesar's legionaries crossed upriver from the town because the water was too high to be forded.

Caesar ordered his troops to dig in one hill north of the Pompeian position, and when the defensive position was ready, he moved to capture the intervening hill. However, the Pompeians had the same idea and took possession of the hill first.

As Caesar writes in *Commentarii de Bello Civili,*

The place was craggy in the front and steep on either side, and was so narrow that even three cohorts, drawn up in order of battle, would fill it; but no relief could be sent on the flanks, and the cavalry could be of no service to them when hard pressed....The greatest contest was in this place, which was much to the disadvantage of our troops, both on account of its narrowness, and because they were posted at the foot of the mountain, so that no weapon was thrown at them without effect; yet they exerted their valor and patience, and bore every wound. The enemy's forces were increasing, and cohorts were frequently sent to their aid from the camp through the town, that fresh men might relieve the weary. Caesar was obliged to do the same, and relieve the fatigued by sending cohorts to that post.

Only a concerted uphill charge by Caesar's Legio IX allowed the rest of the command to withdraw from the fight. Both sides, Caesar asserts, thought themselves the winner, although the Pompeians still held the disputed ground. Caesar reported 70 of his men killed in action but put the enemy death toll at more than 200.

Caesar's difficulties only increased when flooding from a severe storm washed out the bridges that his men had repaired; this isolated his legions west of the Sicoris and cut them off from their supply lines, which ran eastward into Transalpine Gaul.

Because Afranius and Petreius had stockpiled much of the available food in the area, foraging proved difficult. The Pompeians also controlled the intact stone bridge across the river at Ilerda, so they were able to cross over to attack a supply train that had been en route to Caesar's camp when it was halted by the impassable river. Indeed, the Pompeians' position seemed so favorable that they sent messages to Rome bragging that Caesar's defeat was imminent.

The Pompeians knew that the river was too high and too swift for Caesar's engineers to attempt to build a bridge. If they did try it under such difficult conditions, Pompeian archers could attack them.

However, this apparent dilemma opened an opportunity for Caesar. Just as he had discovered in 52 BC that the Gauls had learned Roman engineering, so could the Romans learn from the barbarians. Caesar recalled the small boats that the Britanni put together in the field for use in crossing rivers. Describing them in *Commentarii de Bello Civili,* he writes that "first, the keels and ribs were made of light timber, then, the rest of the hulk of the ships was wrought with wicker work, and covered over with hides." In this they were like the buffalo-hide bull boats used by the Plains Indian tribes in North America.

Caesar's legionaries, some of whom had been with him in Britannia, were put to work building a number of these vessels. When they were completed, they were carried 22 miles away, where they were used to transport troops across the river without being seen by the Pompeians. Engineers were also transported to the east bank, so that they could work from both sides out of the sight of the Pompeians. They finished the bridge in two days, which allowed supplies to come west and troops to be shifted eastward.

Caesar's presence on the east side of the Sicoris surprised the Pompeians, who withdrew into their fortified positions. At the same time horsemen from a number of Hispanic tribes approached Caesar to offer their services as auxiliary cavalry. He readily accepted, as their numbers gave Caesar cavalry superiority over the Pompeians.

When Caesar writes that these developments "struck a terror into the enemy," he does so with a measure of hyperbole, but they would certainly have been troubling to Afranius and Petreius. He is right that the two legati were "extremely apprehensive of being entirely cut off from their provisions and forage, because [my command] was very strong in cavalry."

With this in mind they decided to abandon Ilerda and retreat south to the Ebro River, where they would cross using a pontoon bridge constructed with locally scrounged boats. As they moved out, Caesar was able to use his cavalry superiority to harass the rear of their column.

In his description of the action Caesar writes that "sometimes [my men] obliged them to halt, and disordered their ranks; at other times, the enemy facing about, charged with all their cohorts at once, and forced our men to give ground; who, wheeling again as soon as they began to march, failed not to renew the attack.... During these continual skirmishes, in which the enemy were often obliged to halt, in order to disengage their rear, it is easy to perceive that their march could not be very expeditious."

Moving more quickly, Caesar's men were actually able to get ahead of the Pompeian column and thus to attack them from all sides—with archers and cavalry patrols—as they marched.

Though his men smelled victory and pleaded with Caesar for a decisive battle, he replied that he hoped to avoid it. Even when Afranius and Petreius halted to go into battle order, he avoided a fight and kept his horsemen in the hills. His reason was simple. There were Romans on both sides, and he wanted to minimize the shedding of Roman blood.

Nevertheless, when Afranius detached four Hispanic cohorts to capture a particular mountain ahead of Caesar's men, Caesar sent his cavalry to surround them, "and cut them in pieces in sight of both armies."

Caesar could see that he was gradually wearing the Pompeians down. He had intercepted their provisions, and his cavalry attacks were sapping their morale and preventing them from foraging for water in the dry heat of August. The operation was like a moving siege.

The two sides were often within shouting distance, and as they were all Latin speakers, conversations came up. Talk turned to the question of whether Caesar might show mercy to defectors. As Caesar writes, "Their soldiers found frequent opportunities of conversing with our men, and sought out every one his fellow citizen and acquaintance. They began by thanking them for having spared them the day before, owning they were indebted to them for their lives. Afterwards they asked them, if they might trust to Caesar's honor; testifying much grief at being obliged to fight with their countrymen and relations, with whom they were united by the strictest ties."

Caesar observes that "in the judgment of all, [I] was upon the point of amply reaping the fruits of [my] wonted clemency, and everybody applauded [my] late conduct."

However, it was not to be. When he heard what was going on, Afranius angrily attacked his own men with his praetorian guard and Hispanic cavalry, killing every man he suspected of disloyalty. Afterward he tearfully repented such a rash action.

As the days slipped by and the Pompeian march slowed to a crawl, Caesar finally ordered a strong and forceful cavalry attack. He badly mauled the Pompeian rear and then ordered his legions to threaten the column "with an immediate attack."

The idea was to bring the enemy column, and the moving siege itself, to a halt in a place of his careful choosing. Caesar writes, "As they could then neither choose a proper place for a camp, nor continue their march, they were forced to halt where they were, far from any water, and on very disadvantageous ground."

Caesar did not attack them but drew up in battle order as though he was ready to attack. In so doing, his men were also ready to quickly go into pursuit mode if the enemy decided to make a run for it. The Pompeians spent the whole night and the whole next day digging in. Caesar watched and waited as they ran short of water and were forced to kill pack animals in order to eat.

Caesar writes that "at last, having no hope left, and being in want of every thing, wood, water, forage, corn, they demanded an interview, and that it might be, if possible, in some place out of the sight of the soldiers." Caesar denied the latter but agreed to a conference.

When they met on the open plain between the two armies, Afranius told Caesar "with all possible marks of humility and submission" that "having their bodies oppressed by want, and their minds overwhelmed with ignominy, that they therefore acknowledged themselves vanquished, and besought and conjured him, not to make a rigorous use of his victory, but to spare the lives of his unhappy countrymen."

Caesar accepted the surrender, promising that he would "injure no man" if the Pompeian generals disbanded their army and renounced any further active participation in the civil war. In fact, he welcomed a great many of the Pompeian legionaries into his own army.

As for the two Pompeian legions in Hispania Ulterior under the command of Marcus Varro, they surrendered as soon as they heard what Caesar had done and what had happened to the other Pompeian legions.

Varro, like Afranius and Petreius, agreed to disband his army and cease hostilities toward Caesar. None of the three kept his word with respect to supporting Pompey in the civil war. Indeed, after Caesar generously spared their lives, they raced off to join Pompey, though they never again reached the level of command that they enjoyed as the legati of multiple legions in Hispania.

Having neutralized Pompey's army without a leader, Caesar turned eastward, looking for a showdown with the leader without an army.

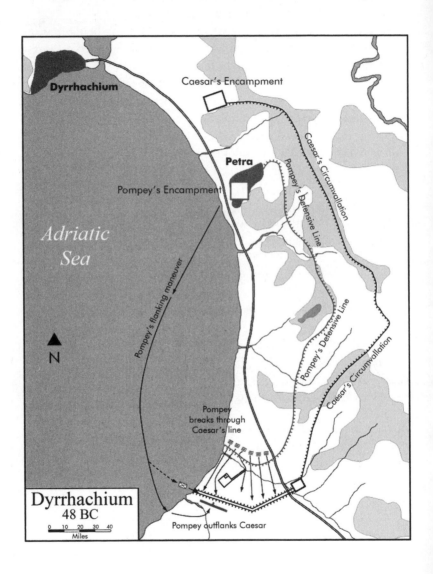

Dyrrhachium

Caesar's Encampment

Petra

Pompey's Encampment

Adriatic
Sea

Pompey's flanking maneuver

Caesar's Circumvallation

Pompey's Defensive Line

Pompey's Defensive Line

Caesar's Circumvallation

N

Pompey
breaks through
Caesar's line

Pompey outflanks Caesar

Dyrrhachium
48 BC

0 10 20 30 40
Miles

CHAPTER 17

From Massilia to Dyrrhachium

WHILE JULIUS CAESAR WAS IN HISPANIA THROUGH THE SUMMER OF 49 BC, the siege of the well-provisioned Massilia continued. Gaius Trebonius assaulted the city from the land, while a naval force loyal to Caesar lay offshore to intercept Pompeian ships trying to reach the port. The fleet was commanded by Decimus Junius Brutus Albinus, the same legatus who had commanded Caesar's fleet off Brittany in the crucial defeat of the Veneti in 56 BC. While Pompey had overall naval superiority in the Mediterranean, most of his fleet was in the east. This and the skill of Brutus and his small fleet allowed Caesar's naval assets to operate more effectively in the waters off Massilia than elsewhere.

Opposing Brutus was the Pompeian fleet under the legatus Lucius Domitius Ahenobarbus, whom Caesar had defeated and pardoned at Corfinium earlier in the year, along with Lucius Nasidius, who commanded a fleet of 16 warships with brass ramming beaks.

Caesar acknowledges that Brutus's seamen and ships were not the best, writing in *Commentarii de Bello Civili* that "our men, not having such expert seamen, or skillful pilots, for they had been hastily drafted from the merchant ships, and were not yet acquainted even with the names of the rigging, were moreover impeded by the heaviness and slowness of our vessels, which having been built in a hurry and of green timber, were not so easily maneuvered." Despite these handicaps, Caesar's fleet nevertheless managed to hold its own, outmaneuvering and boarding the Pompeian vessels, slaying their crews, and sinking the ships. Brutus was also able to address his inferiority of numbers by capturing some Pompeian ships in the ongoing naval skirmishes.

Of the land battle, Caesar notes that Trebonius brought in materiel from throughout Transalpine Gaul to build fortifications and siege engines, and that he built a siege wall that was 80 feet high. Caesar also notes that Trebonius was able to turn back Pompeian attempts to sally forth from the city.

When the Pompeians and Massilians tried to burn his siege engines, Trebonius had his engineers build a six-story brick turret 30 feet wide and about 60 feet from the city wall; the turret functioned as a fixed siege engine as well as a place of refuge for his troops. From this they extended a movable platform to the city wall. Built of heavy timbers, it had a roof that was "covered with tiles and mortar, to secure it against fire, which might be thrown from the wall."

Attempts by Massilia's defenders to burn this platform, or to smash it with rocks dropped from higher towers, failed. Trebonius sent his men across to attack the enemy walls with crowbars, and soon they had collapsed one of the city's turrets.

Caesar writes, "The enemy, distressed at the sudden fall of the turret, surprised at the unforeseen calamity, awed by the wrath of the gods, and dreading the pillage of their city, rush all together out of the gate unarmed, with their temples bound with fillets, and suppliantly stretch out their hands to the officers and the army. At this uncommon occurrence, the whole progress of the war was stopped.... They saw that their city was taken, our works completed, and their tower undermined, therefore they desisted from a defense."

At this Trebonius ordered his troops to halt and not rush the undefended city. Caesar had given him strict orders "not to suffer the town to be taken by storm, lest the soldiers, too much irritated both by abhorrence of their revolt, by the contempt shown to them, and by their long labor, should put to the sword all the grownup inhabitants, as they threatened to do. And it was with difficulty that they were then restrained from breaking into the town, and they were much displeased, because they imagined that they were prevented by Trebonius from taking possession of it."

Following Caesar's orders, Trebonius consistently resisted the temptation to storm the town. Even when some of the Massilians broke the truce, set fire to his platform and attacked his men, he reacted only defensively. After his men had killed a number of the attackers, Trebonius might have launched a counterattack against Massilia, but he ordered his men to force the remaining attackers back inside and to halt there. When it finally became clear to Trebonius that the city had surrendered for good, he ordered his men to begin working with the Massilians to rebuild the city.

Shortly thereafter, in September, as Caesar was marching back from Hispania with his legions, a formal surrender took place.

Julius Caesar returned to Rome in October 49 BC to find that the Senate had once again embraced him and had begun to bestow honors upon him. Being a winner contributed to his political support, but his endeavoring to spare Roman lives and pardoning his enemies after defeating them made him widely popular.

He was appointed dictator, a position he renounced less than two weeks later when he was elected consul, the post that he craved most. He now had legitimate political power to match his immense military power.

During the first year of the civil war, Caesar had consolidated his power in Rome, as well as in the western Mediterranean, but the showdown with Pompey in Epirus was still unavoidable.

Caesar left Rome in January 48 BC, one year after he had crossed the Rubicon with a single legion. Back then he was an enemy of the state. Now he was consul and marched at the head of 12 legions, although he had only enough shipping to take seven across the Adriatic Sea to Epirus.

He embarked from Brindisi, making his move from Italy to Epirus in the winter when Pompey least suspected it. Indeed, this was vital to Caesar's strategy because Pompey held naval superiority in the Adriatic and Ionian Seas, having acquired assets from the navies of all the eastern Mediterranean states, including Bithynia,

Cilicia, Phoenicia, Syria, and even Egypt. This fleet, commanded by Caesar's old colleague Marcus Calpurnius Bibulus, might have been mobilized to sink the fleet of transports carrying the legions to Epirus, but it wasn't. Bibulus was not vigilant to the unexpected and did not see what was going on. Caesar slipped through unimpeded.

Once he landed, however, Caesar found himself in a tenuous situation, both logistically and tactically. His supply lines ran across more than a hundred miles of open sea that he did not control. Pompey had also increased his strength from five to nine legions through the addition of veteran Roman troops who had settled in Sicily, Crete, and Macedonia, as well as auxiliary troops who had been enlisted locally. These were dug in to defensive positions that he had been working on, and provisioning, for the better part of a year. As Caesar grumbles in *Commentarii de Bello Civili,* Pompey had "a year's respite to provide forces, during which he was not engaged in war, nor employed by an enemy."

Caesar had landed in the vicinity of the Gulf of Oricum (now Vlores Bay in Albania) and marched to the city of Oricum, where Pompey had installed Lucius Torquatus as governor. As Caesar writes of Oricum, "a garrison of Parthinians in it, endeavored to shut the gates and defend the town, and ordered the Greeks to man the walls, and to take arms. But as they refused to fight against the power of the Roman people, and as the citizens made a spontaneous attempt to admit Caesar, despairing of any assistance, [Torquatus] threw open the gates, and surrendered himself and the town to Caesar, and was preserved safe from injury by him."

Pompey, meanwhile, had fortified another important coastal city, Dyrrhachium, now Durrës, Albania, about 60 miles to the north, as his base of operations.

Despite Caesar's plan for an early battle, the initial fighting in the spring of 48 BC was limited to skirmishing as Caesar foraged for food, which was hard to find. Caesar describes this part of the Epirus coastal region as being "rough and mountainous," adding that "the people commonly import what grain they use."

In April, Mark Antony was able to bring an additional four of Caesar's legions across the Adriatic, eluding the Pompeian naval blockade during a storm. He landed about 40 miles north of Dyrrhachium.

This put the other armies into motion. When Pompey learned of the landing, he moved to attack Antony before he could link up with Caesar. Meanwhile, Caesar was moving north but marching inland, in order to give a wide berth to Pompey's stronghold at Dyrrhachium.

Despite having to travel farther, Caesar was able to reach Antony before Pompey and was also approached by representatives of the Greek states of Thessaly and Aetolia. They sought an alliance with him if he would protect them. Caesar agreed, if these states would supply him with provisions. This was a vital logistical consideration because food was hard to scrounge on the rugged coast, and the naval superiority enjoyed by the Pompeians made it difficult for Caesar to depend on being resupplied from Italy.

To placate his new friends, Caesar sent his inexperienced Legio XXVII under Lucius Cassius Longinus to Thessaly with 200 cavalry, and Gaius Calvisius Sabinus with five cohorts and a few horsemen to Aetolia. Caesar also dispatched Gneius Domitius Calvinus to Macedonia with the veteran Legiones XI and XII when Caesar learned that Pompey's ally, Scipio, was marching through Macedonia on his way west with two legions.

When Scipio's scout informed him of what Caesar was doing, Scipio diverted from his march into Macedonia to attack Cassius in Thessaly. In so doing, Scipio left Marcus Favonius with eight cohorts to defend the crossing of the Haliacmon River, which separates Macedonia from Thessaly. As Cassius took to the mountains to evade Scipio, Domitius moved against Favonius.

With this turn of events Scipio reversed his march again to reinforce Favonius. As Caesar writes, "The vigilance of Domitius saved Cassius, and the expedition of Scipio, Favonius."

For the next several days Scipio and Domitius each maneuvered for terrain favorable for combat, and while there was frequent serious cavalry skirmishing, both sides maintained a defensive posture.

Meanwhile, Caesar was maneuvering for his own major battle against Pompey. By making a difficult and circuitous march through the coastal mountains toward Pompey's major supply center at Dyrrhachium, Caesar hoped to lure his rival into a decisive fight. As Caesar successfully reached the coast south of Dyrrhachium, cutting Pompey off from his supply base, Pompey ordered his men to dig in at a smaller port called Petra, which was only about two miles from Caesar's position. Describing the lay of the land, Caesar writes that "round Pompey's camps there were several high and rough hills," on which Caesar "raised strong forts... drawing a fortification from one fort to another, as the nature of each position allowed."

Caesar states that his purpose was "to prevent Pompey from foraging, and thereby render his [cavalry] ineffectual in the operations of the war; and... to lessen his reputation, on which he saw he depended greatly, among foreign nations, when a report should have spread throughout the world that he was blockaded."

Because he was unable to reach Dyrrhachium, Pompey's logistics were now stretched, as Caesar's had been earlier. In *Commentarii de Bello Civili* Caesar seems to believe that Pompey was reluctant to engage in a decisive battle, and that threatening Dyrrhachium was necessary to goad Pompey into a fight. As Caesar puts it, Pompey was unwilling "to leave the sea and Dyrrhachium, because he had lodged his materiel there, his weapons, arms, and engines; and supplied his army with corn from it by his ships; nor was he able to put a stop to Caesar's works without hazarding a battle, which at that time he had determined not to do."

Pompey was, according to Caesar, "left but to adopt the last resource, namely, to possess himself of as many hills as he could, and cover as great an extent of country as possible with his troops, and divide [my] forces as much as possible."

The two armies spent the summer of 48 BC in constant skirmishing, as their respective engineers built ever-expanding siege lines that eventually stretched for nearly 20 miles. Caesar occupied the high ground, trying to keep Pompey contained.

With his back to the sea, Pompey extended his defensive line in order to force Caesar to stretch his circumvallation thinner and thinner. As it was stretched, Pompey hoped for breaks that he could exploit.

Of course, by controlling the high ground, Caesar was able to control the flow of streams on which the Pompeians depended for freshwater. While other supplies could be brought into Petra by ship, the heat of the summer made lack of water a critical problem for Pompey, exacerbated by the stench of livestock that had died of thirst. Meanwhile, Caesar's men ate barley and chara roots while waiting for the corn to ripen in the fields.

Gradually, slingers and archers inflicted ever-higher death tolls on both sides, and the small-unit skirmishing evolved into larger and bloodier battles. When Pompey forced Caesar back in one part of the line, he bragged to those around him of a triumph.

In turn, Caesar launched a counterattack, spearheaded by Legio IX, which was commanded by Mark Antony. By shifting forces within his confined space, Pompey was able to meet and blunt Antony's counterattack and attack elsewhere on the line. Caesar reports six engagements in one day, three among the fortresses on the circumvallation and three close to Dyrrhachium.

A turning point came a few days later when two Allobroges cavalry leaders among Caesar's auxiliaries were caught padding their payrolls with wages for nonexistent troops. To escape disciplinary action they defected to Pompey, taking vital information regarding Caesar's strengths and weaknesses.

Using this, Pompey launched a massive, two-part assault against Caesar's line on the morning of July 9, 48 BC. One part involved a concentrated attack across the natural barrier of a streambed that lay in the no-man's land between the respective lines at the southern end of the front near the sea. As seen in the map on page 150, the second aspect of Pompey's attack entailed bringing troops in from his headquarters at Petra by boat. These made an amphibious landing behind Caesar's lines in the same sector as the strike through no-man's land. Pompey thus succeeded in outflanking the southern end of Caesar's line, trapping his legionaries between a hammer and anvil. Doing so, they showed no mercy. With the Pompeians having outflanked a key part of the line, Caesar's position began to unravel.

Caesar realized from the outset that he was losing the battle. It was clear to him that Pompey had the momentum. He even acknowledges that the morale of his troops was collapsing. He goes on to say that the centurions could "neither persuade [Caesar's legionaries] to rally, nor were able themselves to withstand the enemy's charge. The [same thing] happened to a second detachment; insomuch that the several supplies sent, by catching the general terror, served only to add to the confusion and danger; for the multitude of runaways rendered the retreat the more difficult.... The Pompeians made great slaughter of our men."

Caesar's efforts to rally his troops were fruitless. As he later lamented, "If [I] seized any by the arm, they struggled till they got away. If [I] laid hold of the colors, they left them in [my] hands. Not a man could be prevailed on to face about." He acknowledged losing 960 men and 30 officers, but there were probably many more.

A bitter, chagrinned Caesar notes that after he perceived the loss he had sustained, "and that Pompey had forced the lines, being able to forage, and having an easy communication with the sea; [I] quitted [the siege line] project, which had proved unsuccessful."

Caesar retreated, pulling his supply train and his troops out of his line under cover of darkness. He had been crushed. It was probably the worst defeat ever inflicted upon Julius Caesar.

Caesar could see this, but Pompey did not.

Assuming and fearing that Caesar's retreat was merely a tactical withdrawal to lead him into an ambush, Pompey simply moved his own fixed line forward a short distance and dug in again. When a Pompeian cavalry contingent was ambushed and slaughtered by one of Caesar's withdrawing cavalry commands, it only confirmed Pompey's misinterpretation.

One can imagine Caesar, on a hilltop, watching his beaten legions retreat, and the armies of Pompey refusing to destroy them as they could have done so easily. Caesar was left to shake his head as his men escaped, musing that the victory had been Pompey's, but he had failed to take what fate had gifted him.

In his biography of Pompey, Plutarch writes that "Pompey made a brilliant fight and at last routed Caesar's whole force and killed 2,000 of them. He did not, however, force his way into their camp with the fugitives, either because he could not, or because he feared to do so, and this led Caesar to say to his friends: 'Today victory would have been with the enemy if they had had a victor in command.'"

CHAPTER 18

The Battle of Pharsalus

IN THE WARM SUMMER OF 48 BC POMPEY THE GREAT WOKE UP ON the morning after the Battle of Dyrrhachium to learn that the army of Julius Caesar was not camped a few hundred yards away on the surrounding hills but gone. Pompey had defeated Caesar but had failed to appreciate how successfully. He had assumed that Caesar withdrew a short distance in order to trap him, but instead Caesar had undertaken a full-blown retreat. Pompey had soundly defeated Caesar, but he had failed to destroy his retreating army.

Caesar, meanwhile, was on the march, heading inland, eastward into Thessaly to link up with his legatus Domitius Calvinus. Domitius was camped with Legiones XI and XII near the Haliacmon River to prevent the army of Scipio from reaching the coast of Epirus to join Pompey.

Caesar met Domitius on the border of Epirus and Thessaly and permitted his legionaries to plunder the nearby town of Gomphi, an opportunity rare during the civil war. The reason was apparently to improve their sagging morale.

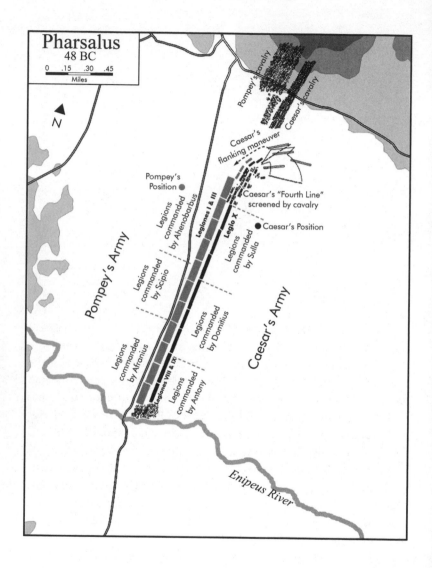

Pharsalus
48 BC

0   .15   .30   .45
Miles

N

Pompey's cavalry

Caesar's cavalry

Caesar's flanking maneuver

Pompey's Position

Caesar's "Fourth Line" screened by cavalry

Legions commanded by Ahenobarbus

Legiones I & III

Legio X

Caesar's Position

Legions commanded by Sulla

Legions commanded by Scipio

Pompey's Army

Legions commanded by Domitius

Legions commanded by Afranius

Legiones VIII & IX

Legions commanded by Antony

Caesar's Army

Enipeus River

As the campaign entered the next phase, Pompey had two distinct choices. The first was to use his unchallenged naval superiority which gave him the capability to ship his legions back across the Adriatic, returning to Italy where the pro-Caesar faction was defenseless. Pompey could have marched into Rome unopposed, isolating Caesar indefinitely in Greece. Pompey's second choice was to pursue, and hope to destroy, Caesar, making up for the monumental blunder at Dyrrhachium.

Pompey chose the second option. His next decision was how to best win against Caesar's forces.

He could easily have avoided a battle and waited Caesar out. Pompey had excellent logistical support, with supplies readily available wherever he turned, while Caesar was living from meal to meal on whatever his foragers could scrounge. Sooner or later Caesar's troops would have been at the end of their provisions.

Or Pompey could have done what many of his subordinate leaders favored: force a battle in which his numerical advantage would result, they assumed, in Caesar's defeat.

Pompey chose battle.

Shortly after Caesar had joined forces with Domitius, Pompey reached Thessaly by way of a more northern route and linked up with Scipio. All sides now prepared to fight, and battle lines were drawn.

The rematch between Caesar and Pompey came about one month after Dyrrhachium. The place was just north of the Enipeus River in southern Thessaly, near Pharsalus (also called Pharsalia), which is now the Greek town of Farsala.

While the Battle of Dyrrhachium had been preceded by months of digging, building, and skirmishing, the Battle of Pharsalus was a classic field battle between two forces. Pompey did initially start to dig in at an advantageous location on a hill at the foot of a mountain, but Caesar continued to maneuver, so Pompey decided to meet his rival in the open.

Caesar estimated the size of the respective commands at 22,000 legionaries and 1,000 cavalry for his side, while Pompey had 45,000 legionaries and 7,000 cavalry. These numbers were augmented by several thousand auxiliaries. Both sides had Germanic and Gallic auxiliaries, mainly horsemen, while Pompey had infantry troops from Greece and from throughout the eastern expanse of Rome's dominions. His armies included Macedonians as well as Athenians and Spartans. He had troops from Cilicia, Crete, Syria, Rhodes, and even Armenia. King Ariarathes of Cappadocia had also joined Pompey with some of his troops.

Both Caesar and Pompey organized their legions into three contingents, each three lines deep.

On Caesar's side the left wing (against the steep banks of the Enipeus) was comprised of Legiones VIII and IX, which had borne the brunt of the fighting at Dyrrhachium; the commander was Mark Antony. The center was under Domitius, while the right was under Publius Cornelius Sulla. Caesar himself was on the right side with Sulla and Legio X, long his favorite legion.

On Pompey's side the left wing (opposite Caesar) was comprised of Legiones I and III, commanded by Lucius Domitius Ahenobarbus. The center was comprised of the two Syrian legions under Scipio. The right wing (opposite Antony and next to the river), included troops from Cilicia and Hispania, and was commanded by Lucius Afranius, whom Caesar had pardoned in Hispania in 49 BC. Marcus Petreius, also pardoned in Hispania, was present among Pompey's officers.

Pompey was with Ahenobarbus, and Caesar considered that Pompey was actually in direct command on the left. Adjacent to the left wing was the Pompeian cavalry contingent, commanded by Titus Atius Labienus, who had been one of Caesar's most loyal and capable lieutenants during the Gallic Wars. In his own recollections of these battles, Caesar notes the bitter irony of seeing his former subordinates on the opposing side but is determined to defeat them.

Labienus apparently had a low opinion of Legiones IX and X and the rest of Caesar's army. According to Caesar, Labienus told Pompey, to "think not that these are the legions which conquered Gaul and Germany. I was present in all those battles, and can, of my own knowledge, affirm, that but a very small part of that army now remains; great numbers have been killed, as must of necessity happen, in such a variety of conflicts. . . . The veterans, in whom consisted the main strength of the army, perished all in the two defeats at Dyrrhachium."

For his opening gambit Pompey planned to use the cavalry commanded by the cocky Labienus to outflank the ranks of Caesar's infantry. Pompey had positioned his legions so that the river covered his right, while Labienus operated on the left.

In his *Commentarii de Bello Civili* Caesar paints a particularly colorful picture of the way his own men marched forth early on that warm summer morning. He writes of Gaius Crastinus, "a man of distinguished courage, who the year before, had been first centurion of Legio X. This brave officer, as soon as the signal was given, calling to those next him: 'Follow me,' said he, 'you that were formerly under my command, and acquit yourselves of the duty you owe to your general. This one battle more will crown the work, by restoring him to his proper dignity, and us to the enjoyment of our freedom.'"

Turning to Caesar, Crastinus reportedly said, "This day you shall be satisfied with my behavior, and whether I live or die, I will take care to deserve your commendations."

With that Crastinus led the march of Caesar's right wing toward the Pompeian lines.

While Caesar's legions all advanced together, Pompey's held fast. One reason may have been that he feared that his international contingents might get out of step with his Roman troops, adversely affecting the cohesiveness of the lines. Another theory is that Pompey hoped Caesar's men would be tired by their forward march.

Caesar writes that his legionaries, "perceiving the enemy did not stir, . . . halted, of their own accord, in the midst of their career; and having taken a moment's breath, put themselves, a second time, in motion; marched up in good order, flung their javelins, and then betook themselves to their swords. Nor did Pompey's men act with less presence of mind: for they sustained our attack, kept their ranks, bore the discharge of our darts: and having launched their own, immediately had recourse to their swords."

By now Pompey had released Labienus and the cavalry to flank the men on Caesar's right wing. Because Labienus's troops outnumbered Caesar's cavalry by as much as 7 to 1, Labienus confidently expected a rout. Instead, Caesar's cavalry melted away, and the Pompeian horsemen found themselves facing ranks of infantry with spears. Caesar had pulled six cohorts out of the legions and had hidden them behind a screen of cavalry as a reserve force. This "fourth line" was positioned at an angle, adjacent to, not behind, the other three lines.

Though Labienus had earlier mocked the inexperience of Caesar's men, his own contingent had a similar flaw. Their strength was in their superior numbers, but this turned out to also be a weakness, as few of the cavalrymen had the practical experience of operating as part of a tactical unit this large.

Their surprised reaction to the spear-wielding cohorts was evasive action that melted into a swirling mass of confusion. This was only multiplied by the huge numbers of the Pompeian cavalry. As his huge cavalry turned into a panicked sea of stumbling horses and falling riders, perhaps Labienus had time to appreciate the irony of his earlier assertion.

As Caesar happily tells it, the fourth-line cohorts "fell on the enemy's cavalry with such fury that they not only drove them from the field of battle, but even compelled them to seek refuge in the highest mountains. The archers and slingers, deprived of their protection, were soon after cut to pieces. Meanwhile the six cohorts, not content with this success, wheeled round upon the enemy's left wing, and began to charge it in the rear."

Caesar's legions, amazingly disciplined after their near-collapse at Dyrrhachium, managed to break down the forward line of Pompey's legions. When this line collapsed, it did so inward against the second, allowing Caesar's men to march through and over the top of the Pompeian lines.

Part of the reason for the collapse may have been that the international contingents, which were between the Pompeian legions like mortar between bricks, had failed. When Caesar's legions struck, a failure of communication—few, if any, of Pompey's international troops could speak Latin—dissolved the polyglot units into bewilderment, and they got in the way of Pompey's more disciplined Romans.

The scene was reminiscent of the communication failure and collapse of the international contingents within the Persian army of Darius III. In his epic loss to Alexander the Great at Gaugamela in 331 BC, Darius had lost command and control of a huge army comprised of units from throughout the Persian Empire that had no common language or common battlefield organization. Though Alexander was greatly outnumbered, he had excellent communications and an army that was used to operating as a unit.

Pompey had already committed all three of his lines, and when the swirl of disarray began, unit integrity was lost. Caesar, meanwhile, held his own third line back, in part to support the fourth line facing the Pompeian cavalry and in part so as to have a fresh line to throw into the fight on the main battlefield. Caesar deftly committed his third line at just the right moment, when the momentum of his legions needed a push to send the Pompeians sprawling. The third line mopped the battlefield with the remaining Pompeians.

According to Caesar, the battle was essentially over by noon. As Caesar writes,

> Pompey, seeing his cavalry routed, and that part of the army on which he chiefly depended, put into disorder, despaired of being able to restore the battle, and quitted the field. Repairing immediately to his camp, he said aloud, to the centurions, who guarded the praetorian gate, so as all the soldiers might hear him: "Take care of the camp, and defend it vigorously in case of an attack. I go to visit the other gates, and give orders for their defense." This said, he retired to his tent, despairing of success, yet waiting the event.

Even Plutarch, in his biography of Pompey, tells a similar story. He writes that "after his infantry was thus routed, and when, from the cloud of dust which he saw, Pompey conjectured the fate of his cavalry, what thoughts passed through his mind it were difficult to say; but he was most like a man bereft of sense and crazed, who had utterly forgotten that he was Pompey the Great, and without a word to any one, he walked slowly off to his camp....In such a state of mind he went to his tent and sat down speechless."

Some Pompeians retreated to their camp, others to the hills. Caesar instructed his men to pursue and destroy the retreating stragglers, something that Pompey had failed to do a month earlier at

Dyrrhachium. According to Caesar, although "the weather [was] extremely hot...they cheerfully complied with [these] orders."

When the Pompeians who retreated into the nearby mountains saw that there was no water there to support them in making a stand, they continued north toward the town of Larissa with Caesar's men in close pursuit. The Pompeians surrendered after being surrounded.

According to Caesar's probably exaggerated numbers, he lost only 200 legionaries and 30 centurions—including the gallant Crastinus—while the Pompeians suffered 15,000 men killed in action and 24,000 taken as prisoners in a formal surrender that took place the following day.

As Caesar tells it, they "delivered up their arms; humbly imploring his goodness, and suing for mercy." In turn, he gave them their lives and forbade his soldiers "to offer them any violence, or to take any thing from them."

The Battle of Pharsalus is often described as Caesar's greatest victory. Indeed, such a description was already being used throughout the Mediterranean region within weeks of the battle. If it was not, it was second only to Alesia.

The battle has also been called a "clash of Titans" between Caesar and Pompey, but even before it was over, Pompey was no longer titanic in stature. As the battle still raged, he shed his crimson cape, his general's uniform, and sneaked away wearing a common legionary's cloak.

Pompey escaped first to Larissa, accompanied by a gaggle of Optimate politicians and senators who had been hangers-on in his court through the previous year. From there they made it to the coast—Caesar writes that they robbed a bank en route to fund their flight and hitched a ride on a merchant ship bound for Egypt by way of Cyprus.

Afranius, Labienus, and Scipio also escaped, running west to the Adriatic coast, where they also caught a ship bound for Africa. Ahenobarbus was killed trying to escape.

When he learned that Pompey had escaped, Caesar was determined to give chase in order to prevent him from raising another army and continuing the civil war. Caesar sent Mark Antony back to

Rome, and Domitius to Syria with three legions, while Caesar took Legio VI and headed for Egypt by way of Ephesus in Asia Minor.

Meanwhile, another civil war—a squabble between a pair of teen-aged siblings—was simmering in Egypt. The pharaoh, Ptolemy XII, had recently died and had been succeeded by his children. These were Ptolemy XIII, who was in his early teens, and Cleopatra VII, who was in her late teens. The brother and sister had been married to one another in a royal wedding so they could serve jointly. They had inherited the throne of a line of Greco-Egyptian pharaohs going back to Ptolemy I, a lieutenant Alexander the Great had installed in office in 305 BC.

Egged on by his advisers—especially Pothinus the eunuch, who managed the young king's affairs—and jealous of his charismatic sister's popularity, Ptolemy XIII had deposed Cleopatra. He and his counselors were ruling Egypt when Pompey's ship arrived off Alexandria about a month after Pharsalus.

Pompey's request for political asylum put young Ptolemy in a quandary. He had also received the news that Caesar, the victor in the epic Battle of Pharsalus, was headed for Alexandria. The last thing that Ptolemy XIII and his nervous courtiers wanted or needed in the fall of 48 BC was to be on the bad side of Julius Caesar. Plutarch also relates that Ptolemy owed the Romans a great deal of money.

When Pompey reached Egypt, he was promptly murdered on orders from Pothinus and Ptolemy. As Pompey's wife watched from offshore, his head was chopped off and his body burned in a bonfire on the beach. One of the assassins was a former Roman centurion turned Egyptian general named Achillas, who now commanded Ptolemy's army.

When Caesar arrived, Ptolemy gave him Pompey's severed head and his signet ring in a grand gesture that Caesar tearfully rebuffed. Pompey was, after all, Caesar's former colleague and son-in-law.

CHAPTER 19

The Conquering Hero and the Queen of the Nile

JULIUS CAESAR, THE MOST POWERFUL MAN IN THE KNOWN WORLD, passed the autumn days of 48 BC in Alexandria, the greatest city to bear the name of the greatest of conquerors, Alexander the Great, Caesar's one true hero and role model. While in the city Caesar also paid his respects at Alexander's royal sarcophagus.

With Pompey dead and his armies badly mauled, Caesar's Civil War entered a new phase. Pompey's lieutenants would continue to challenge Caesar, but for the moment he appeared to believe it was all over. It was not, but he no longer had a challenger who was his equal, as Pompey had once been.

Caesar now found himself preoccupied with playing referee in the petty internecine squabble between Ptolemy XIII and Cleopatra VII, Ptolemy's wife and sister. Caesar sagely recommended arbitration, that is, until he met Cleopatra. She was, by the various accounts written of her, the most beautiful woman in the world or the most beautiful woman in all history—or both. She was, at the very least, an extremely attractive young woman.

Despite a three-decade age difference, Caesar fell madly in love with her, and she seemed to return the sentiment. Either that, or to serve her political goals she shrewdly curried the affections of the most powerful man in the world. Needless to say, Caesar no longer favored a mediated settlement in the dispute about Egypt's throne.

When Caesar openly backed his young lover for the throne, he did so with the full weight of his prestige but at a great disadvantage militarily. While Caesar had brought only a small number of troops with him to Alexandria, Ptolemy and Pothinus were backed by the Egyptian army commanded by Achillas.

In his *Commentarii de Bello Civili,* Caesar writes that Achillas's army consisted of two legions of men, "many of whom were originally Romans, brought into the country by Gabinius, when he came to settle Auletes on the throne; and who, having afterwards married and settled in Alexandria, were devoted to the Ptolemaic interest."

As Caesar points out in this passage, the intervention by Roman armies in Egyptian political squabbles was not new, though Rome had traditionally treated Egypt as an associated state, rather than as a dominion. The specific incident to which Caesar refers came in 55 BC, when Pompey had sent Aulus Gabinius with a Roman army to Egypt to support the right to the throne of Ptolemy XII (the father of Ptolemy XIII and Cleopatra). Also known as "Auletes" (the "flute player"), he had been on the throne since 80 BC, though he was not considered legitimate. What had happened was that his predecessor, Ptolemy XI, had been deposed without an heir after murdering his coregent and stepmother Berenice III. At the time, Auletes, the illegitimate son of Ptolemy IX and his Greek mistress, was living in the court of Mithridates VI, the king of Pontus. As the oldest male in the Ptolemy blood line, he was given the job. When his rule was seriously challenged in 55 BC, Roman troops kept him in power. Many Romans had stayed on to form his "Egyptian" army.

Until reinforcements arrived, Caesar was confined to the sidelines in the unrest that gripped Alexandria during December 48 BC, after Caesar made known his backing of Cleopatra. Caesar writes that he "sent to Rhodes, Syria, and Cilicia, for all his fleet; and summoned archers from Crete, and cavalry from Malchus, king of the Nabatheans," but in the meantime the street fighting became so intense that Caesar feared being blocked from access to the sea, and that his own fleet might be captured and used against him. He therefore was forced to scuttle his ships in the harbor by setting them afire. As he writes, "Had Achillas been once master of these vessels, he might have cut [Caesar] off from all communication with the ocean, and consequently from all hopes of receiving supplies of victuals or forces. Thus the Egyptians, in hopes of a complete victory, and the Romans to avoid a certain ruin, exerted themselves with incredible vigor. At length Caesar carried his point, and not only set fire to the vessels above mentioned, but to all that were in the arsenals, after which he passed some troops into the Isle of Pharos."

However, the flames accidentally spread, destroying at least part of the great Library of Alexandria, the fabled repository of the entire world's knowledge.

As Plutarch writes in his biography of Caesar, "When the enemy tried to cut off his fleet, he was forced to repel the danger by using fire, and this spread from the dockyards and destroyed the great library.... And when a battle arose at Pharos [the Lighthouse of Alexandria, one of the Seven Wonders of the ancient world], he sprang from the causeway into a small boat and tried to go to the aid of his men in their struggle, but the Egyptians sailed up against him from every side, so that he threw himself into the sea and with great difficulty escaped by swimming."

When Caesar's reinforcements, including Legio XXXVII, comprised of former Pompeians now led by Domitius Calvinus, did arrive, Caesar was able to recapture all of Alexandria, defeat the forces of Achillas and Cleopatra's other rivals, and install her on the throne. Pothinus was captured and executed, and young Ptolemy drowned while swimming the Nile, perhaps to escape Caesar. Achillas got away with Cleopatra's younger sister, Arsinoe, herself a would-be challenger for the throne. She had Achillas killed at the instigation of a jealous courtier, but she wound up in Roman custody and was sent to Rome in chains.

Caesar and Cleopatra celebrated with a leisurely two-month cruise on the Nile on a honeymoon-like vacation. Though Roman law prohibited Caesar from marrying a non-Roman, this did not curb their lovemaking. She became pregnant and gave birth in June 47 BC to Caesar's son, the only male child that he is believed to have fathered. Because they remained unmarried, the boy was not officially Caesar's heir. However, he became heir to Cleopatra's throne and later ruled as Ptolemy XV Caesar. He was best known, though, as Caesarion, or Little Caesar.

Throughout 48 and into 47 BC, as Caesar was preoccupied with his civil war against Pompey and with Cleopatra's civil war in Egypt, opportunists in Rome's more distant dominions were taking advantage of the distractions.

In the late spring of 47 BC Caesar kissed his young lover goodbye and took his legions eastward to subdue Pharnaces II of Pontus on the shores of the Black Sea. There, Lucius Cornelius Sulla had defeated Mithridates, the father of Pharnaces and host of Ptolemy XII in his youth, in the series of conflicts that had dominated the news during Caesar's youth. Pharnaces II had since taken control of Roman client states from Cappadocia to Armenia, reclaiming his family's former glory.

Pharnaces had not expected Caesar to intervene against him personally, but soon he gave Caesar no choice. Pharnaces had routed Gneius Domitius Calvinus, whom Caesar had assigned to command the legions in that part of the world. Next the arrogant Pharnaces made the mistake of torturing and murdering Roman prisoners.

Caesar, marching with three understrength legions, caught up with Pharnaces near Zela, a hill town in what is now northern Turkey. Caesar then made camp on a hill across the valley from the enemy's hilltop fortifications.

Taking a page from Caesar's own playbook about a good defense's being a good offense, Pharnaces surprised the Romans by counterintuitively abandoning his advantageous high-ground position to run an uphill attack against the Romans' own high ground.

The Pontic warlord achieved an initial surprise attack but was so badly exposed that Caesar quickly overwhelmed and defeated him. The whole campaign was over so quickly that Caesar coined his famous quip, in a letter to Amantius in Rome: "Veni, vidi, vici" (I came, I saw, I conquered).

In his epic *History of Rome* Cassius Dio writes that "Caesar took great pride in this victory—more in fact, than in any other, even though it had not been very brilliant—because on the same day and in the same hour, he had come to the enemy, had seen him, and had conquered him."

Caesar also used the opportunity of his swift victory to mock the memory of Pompey, who had fought extended campaigns in this part of the world to accomplish what Caesar had now done in half a day.

Pharnaces himself got away but was killed by one of his own former governors.

Although he had pacified the eastern Mediterranean, Caesar still faced threats from Pompey supporters in both North Africa and Hispania as well as pressing concerns at home.

Four legions, nominally under the command of Mark Antony, were camped near Rome awaiting bonuses that they had been promised. When they mutinied in the summer of 47 BC, Antony lost control of the situation, and Caesar had to race back to deal with it.

Julius Caesar's situation in Rome was directly analogous to one faced by General Douglas MacArthur two centuries later. In June 1932, at the depths of the Great Depression, more than 15,000 World War I veterans converged on Washington, DC, to demand immediate payment of bonuses that had been awarded as certificates not redeemable for 20 years. Cassius Dio's summary of Caesar's predicament applies to both dilemmas: the legions "caused [Caesar] no slight trouble; for they had expected to receive a great deal, and when they found their rewards inferior to their expectation, though not less, to be sure, than their deserts, they made a disturbance."

President Herbert Hoover ordered MacArthur, then the US Army chief of staff, to use the army to physically remove the "bonus army" when it refused to disperse. Like Caesar in 47 BC, he faced having to use troops against theretofore loyal men who were demanding only what they had been promised. In both cases the money was needed elsewhere: in 1932 it was the projected cost of recovering from the Depression; in 47 BC Caesar needed to finance further military campaigns in Africa and Hispania.

Caesar, unlike MacArthur in 1932, was already a hero to Roman citizens and Roman troops alike. Caesar was able to approach these men armed only with oratory. MacArthur, whose public hero status would not develop until World War II, resorted to guns and tear gas to disperse the bonus army. Though MacArthur rousted the marchers with minimal injuries, the incident cast a dark shadow and was the antithesis of what Caesar was able to accomplish with words. (In 1936 Congress finally passed the Adjusted Compensation Payment Act over President Roosevelt's veto, sanctioning the immediate payment of nearly $2 billion in bonuses for veterans.)

When Caesar arrived and spoke to the crowd of mutinous soldiers, he soon had them calmed down. He famously addressed them as citizens rather than as soldiers, implying that because of their mutiny, they were no longer worthy.

"Why, of course, Quirites [citizens], what you say is right," Caesar said, according to the account by Cassius Dio. "You are naturally weary and worn out with wounds."

Cassius goes on to say that Caesar then

> at once disbanded them all as if he had no further need of them, promising that he would give the rewards in full to such as had served the appointed time. At these words they were struck with alarm both at his intention in general and particularly because he had called them Quirites instead of soldiers; and so, humiliated and fearing they should meet with some severe penalty, they [turned about] and addressed him with many entreaties and offers, promising that they would join his expedition [to Africa] as volunteers and would carry the war through for him by themselves.

In reply Caesar practically taunted them, saying, "I...discharge both you who are present here and all the rest whose years of service have expired; for I...really have no further need of you. Yet even so I...will pay you the rewards, that no one may say that after using you in dangers I...later showed myself ungrateful, even though you were unwilling to join my campaign while perfectly strong in body and able to carry through all the wars that remain."

With the promise of full pay after the African campaign, the embarrassed men acceded, even begging to be included in the upcoming operations. It might have backfired, but it didn't. It was Caesar at his oratorical best. Cassius reminds us that Caesar had taunted them for effect, because they were quite indispensable to him as he sought to end the civil war.

The penultimate campaign of Caesar's civil war would take Roman armies back to the site of Rome's first demonstration of international military prominence in the Punic Wars.

After the Battle of Pharsalus the Optimate generals and political leaders who had sided and fought with the now-dead Pompey congregated with their armies near the site where Carthage once stood. To bring the civil war to a conclusion, Caesar had to defeat and destroy them.

The moral leader of the Optimate opposition to Caesar in North Africa was Marcus Porcius Cato, a long-time political antagonist of Caesar's. As a senator Cato had been renowned for his integrity. With him were the key Pompeian generals who had slipped away from Pharsalus, such as Marcus Petreius, and Titus Labienus, Caesar's former subordinate commander. In overall command of the Optimate army was Scipio, who had commanded Pompey's center at Pharsalus and whose ancestors had been the prominent generals in the wars against Carthage two centuries earlier.

Caesar's crossing to Africa went poorly. His ships became scattered and landed the legionaries in widely dispersed places. Had Scipio or Labienus met Caesar on the beach with their vast numbers, they would have met him at his most vulnerable, straggling through the breakers with less than a legion to support him. However, the Optimates missed their opportunity, and Caesar managed to locate and pull his six legions into battle order without interference.

The opening battle in the North African campaign took place near Ruspina (now Monastir, Tunisia) on what is now the Gulf of Hammamet, about 100 miles southeast of Carthage, in January 46 BC. During World War II the area would see the climactic North Africa battles of 1943 between the Allies and Field Marshal Erwin Rommel's German Afrika Korps.

Caesar, leading a contingent of 30 cohorts plus cavalry on a foraging mission, was ambushed by a larger force under the command of Labienus and supported by locally enlisted Berber cavalry. This action, unanticipated by Caesar, was a bloody one; he lost an estimated third of his small command, and Labienus had his horse killed out from under him by one of Caesar's javelin throwers. The battle continued until dusk, when the Optimates withdrew.

Though the sides parted without a clear winner, the *Commentarii de Bello Africo* (*Commentaries on the African War*), once attributed to Caesar but now accepted as having been written by someone else, cast Caesar as the victor. The author writes that Caesar

> ordered both [cavalry] and [infantry] to fall at once briskly upon the enemy, and not slacken the pursuit till they had driven them quite beyond the furthest hills, and taken possession of them themselves. Accordingly, upon a signal being given, when the enemy were throwing their javelins in a faint and careless manner, he suddenly charged them with his [cavalry and infantry]; who in a moment driving them from the field, and over the adjoining hill, kept possession of that post for some time, and then retired slowly, in order of battle, to their camp. The enemy, who, in this last attack, had been very roughly handled, then at length retreated to their fortifications.

His actions were nothing but hyperbolic bravado. Caesar was nervous after Ruspina and sent for reinforcements. During the next few weeks Legiones VIII, X, XIII, and XIV all arrived in Africa by way of Sicily to augment Caesar's army, bringing it to ten legions, a closer match with the Optimate numbers.

Meanwhile, Scipio commanded an enormous army, larger even than Pompey's at Pharsalus. Scipio had 12 full-strength legions numbering more than 70,000 men. In addition, the cavalry force, commanded by Labienus, exceeded 14,000 and included many local militias, including a force led by Juba I of the Berber kingdom of Numidia (now Algeria). The force included about 60 war elephants. Plutarch writes that "Scipio was encouraged by these advantages to hazard a decisive battle," although Caesar would initiate the contest.

After a series of smaller skirmishes the climax to the civil war's North African campaign came in April 46 BC at the strategic coastal city of Thapsus (now Ras Dimas, Tunisia) on the Gulf of Hammamet. The fortified city was at the tip of a broad peninsula with water to the north and a coastal swamp to the south. These terrain features would define the battlefield and restrict the maneuvering capability of both sides. Caesar had chosen this place precisely because he knew it would somewhat limit Scipio's ability to make full use of his large numbers.

Caesar opened the operation by engineering multiple siege lines around the city, especially on the south side, in preparation for taking it down. As Cassius Dio relates, "Caesar, when he had got inside the narrowest point, proceeded to dig a ditch and to erect a palisade. The townspeople caused him no trouble, as they were no match for him."

Because of the strategic importance of Thapsus, Scipio could not ignore the siege and was compelled to ride to Caesar's preselected battlefield and engage his legions, which were now positioned on the peninsula leading to the city. Scipio arrived from the inland side with his own and Juba's army, set up camp, and led the legions toward Caesar, approaching from the northwest. According to Cassius, they "undertook in their turn to wall off the neck of the isthmus, where it comes to an end at the mainland, by running palisades and ditches across from both sides." While the legions were digging in, the war elephants were positioned on the leading edge of Scipio's line as a sort of mobile defensive wall.

As Cassius recounts, the Optimate legionaries were still digging in when "Caesar suddenly attacked the men who were with Scipio, and by using slings and arrows from a distance threw the elephants into great confusion. Then as they retreated he not only followed them up, but fell upon the workers unexpectedly and routed them, too; and when they fled into their camp, he dashed in with them and captured it without a blow."

Plutarch explains that "Caesar made his way with inconceivable speed through woody regions which afforded unknown access to [Scipio's position], outflanked some of the enemy, and attacked others in front."

It was a situation much like that back in 57 BC, when the Nervii had attacked Caesar as his legionaries were building their camp. The Romans might easily have been routed, but they rallied. At Thapsus Scipio's men might have rallied, formed into units, and organized a cohesive defense, but they did not. As at Pharsalus, communications probably collapsed amid a polyglot of cohorts that did not share a common language. Then too there was the horror of five dozen stampeding elephants.

When Juba saw what was happening, he might have led his huge cavalry force to outflank Caesar, but Caesar had chosen the battlefield wisely, and there was no spare room in which to maneuver. With no clear way to use his massive corps of horsemen, Juba panicked and ran. As Cassius writes, "Juba, upon seeing this, was so startled and terrified that he ventured neither to come to close quarters with any one nor even to keep the camp under guard; so he fled and hastened homeward.... Caesar, immediately after Juba's flight, captured the palisade."

The anonymous author of *Commentarii de Bello Africo* writes that Caesar,

perceiving that the ardor of his soldiers would admit of no restraint, giving "good fortune" for the word, spurred on his horse, and charged the enemy's front. On the right wing the archers and slingers poured their eager javelins without intermission upon the elephants, and by the noise of their slings and stones, so terrified these animals that turning upon their own men, they trod them down in heaps, and rushed through the half-finished gates of the camp. At the same time the Mauritanian [cavalry], who were in the same wing with the elephants, seeing themselves deprived of their assistance, betook themselves to flight. Whereupon the legions wheeling round the elephants, soon possessed themselves of the enemy's entrenchments, and some few that made great resistance being slain, the rest fled with all expedition to the camp they had quitted the day before.

Plutarch tells a somewhat different story, writing that, at the height of the battle, Caesar had an attack of "his usual sickness," which is interpreted as being one of the six documented epileptic seizures that Caesar suffered during the last decade of his life. "Caesar himself was not in the action, but that, as he was marshaling and arraying his army, his usual sickness laid hold of him, and he, ... at once aware that it was beginning, before his already wavering senses were altogether confounded and overpowered by the malady, was carried to a neighboring tower, where he stayed quietly during the battle."

In the aftermath of the battle Caesar was ruthless and uncharacteristically unforgiving to Optimate legionaries who tried to surrender. He captured the besieged Thapsus and indulged in a massacre of the Optimate troops. As Cassius reports, Caesar "caused great slaughter among all who came in the way of his troops, sparing not even those who came over to his side."

In his biography of Caesar, Plutarch reports that "of the men of consular and praetorial rank who escaped from the battle, some slew themselves at the moment of their capture, and others were put to death by Caesar after capture."

Juba and Marcus Petreius escaped together, but they decided their situation was hopeless and chose to preserve their honor with a duel in which the winner killed himself. Accounts disagree as to who won, but when it was all over, both lay dead. Scipio also got away and was attempting to reach Hispania when he was cornered by a naval force loyal to Caesar. Scipio committed suicide to avoid capture and humiliation. Of the senior Optimate commanders at Thapsus, only Labienus escaped.

Cassius Dio writes that after the battle, "Caesar brought the rest of the cities [of North Africa] to terms, meeting with no opposition; and taking over the Numidians, he reduced them to the status of subjects."

Cato had remained in his villa in Utica, on the Mediterranean coast west of Carthage, and missed the battle entirely. When he heard that Caesar had decimated the Optimate army at Thapsus, Cato too decided that the only way out was with a blade.

As Plutarch writes, "Being eager to take Cato alive, Caesar hastened towards Utica...but he learned that Cato had made away with himself, and he was clearly annoyed, though for what reason is uncertain. At any rate, he said: 'Cato, I...begrudge thee thy death; for thou didst begrudge me the preservation of thy life.'"

Caesar had hoped to make the magnanimous gesture of sparing Cato's life, but he had been cheated of that by Cato himself.

The Battle of Thapsus, like Pharsalus, was a decisive defeat of a major army by outnumbered, but better disciplined, legions led by Julius Caesar. The end of the civil war was in sight. Between the totality of his victory, and his uncharacteristic massacre of higher-ranking survivors, few were left to challenge Caesar.

CHAPTER 20

The Battle of Munda and the End of the Civil War

IN JULY 46 BC, JULIUS CAESAR RETURNED TO ROME IN TRIUMPH, having defeated much of the remaining resistance to his rule, and having stared at the dead bodies of Scipio and Cato.

The Senate declared Caesar dictator of Rome, granting him an unprecedented term of absolute power for ten years. Under Roman law dictatorships were granted for periods not to exceed six months, and only in extraordinary circumstances. Most dictators quickly resigned. Indeed, Caesar himself had resigned his previous dictatorship after a few days. This time the rules were waived for Rome's favorite conquering hero. He quickly set about enacting laws favorable to the Populare point of view, which endeared him even more to the masses in the Roman Republic.

Meanwhile, his achievements in North Africa, and those that had gone before it, resulted in his being honored by the Senate and people with not one but four official Triumphs. Caesar had received a Triumph previously for his Hispanic campaign in 61 BC, and Pompey had received three in his lifetime. Now Caesar was honored with four consecutive Triumphs marking his victorious campaigns in Gaul, Egypt, Pontus, and finally in North Africa. The latter officially recognized his defeat of Juba. Celebrating his defeat of Scipio and Cato, who were Romans, would have been bad form.

For the parade marking the Triumph over Gaul of 52 BC, the great Gallic leader Vercingetorix was taken out of prison to march in chains. Afterward he was killed, albeit not publicly. According to Cassius Dio, Arsinoe, the younger sister and rival of Cleopatra, was also paraded in chains, but she was not executed.

As Plutarch writes in his biography of Caesar, "After the Triumphs, Caesar gave his soldiers large gifts and entertained the people with banquets and spectacles, feasting them all at one time on twenty thousand dining-couches, and furnishing spectacles of gladiatorial and naval combats in honor of his daughter Julia, long since dead."

Even as all this was going on in the capital, the opposition was regrouping in Hispania, where Caesar's military career had begun. After Thapsus the remnants of the armies that had once sided with Pompey and Scipio had rallied in Hispania, making it the last bastion of the Optimates who opposed Caesar. Titus Labienus had escaped there after Thapsus, and with him were Publius Attius Varus, as well as Sextus and Gnaeus Pompeius, the sons of Pompey himself. Gnaeus took the lead role, forming a substantial army of 13 legions, plus numerous auxiliary forces. When Gaius Trebonius, Caesar's commander in this province, proved unable to deal with them, Caesar was compelled to personally lead what would be the final campaign of the civil war.

He assembled eight legions, including the veteran Legiones V and X, as well as newly manned Legiones III and VI, and marched westward in the last weeks of 46 BC, traveling 1,500 miles in less than a month. Among his subordinate officers for the operation were Marcus Agrippa and Caesar's teenaged great-nephew Gaius Octavius Thurinus (Octavian), the grandson of Julia.

Caesar's speedy arrival should have allowed him to launch an immediate attack against the army of the Pompeius brothers, but he found himself drawn into a winter campaign comprised of a succession of smaller, but bloody, skirmishes reminiscent of his winter campaigns in Gaul. He also found himself stalemated in a siege of Corduba (now Cordoba), the capital of Hispania Ulterior, which had become the stronghold for the Pompeians.

These actions combined to gradually sap Caesar's momentum, which was what Gnaeus Pompeius hoped to accomplish. He wanted to avoid, or at least delay, the type of major field battle against Caesar that had been the senior Pompey's downfall. However, there was growing discontent within Gnaeus Pompeius's ranks, and he feared desertions to Caesar's side if the campaign was not brought to a climax soon. With this in mind he began preparations for a decisive contest. The date would be March 17, 45 BC; the battlefield would be the plains near the hilltop town of Munda, probably located near the present Spanish town of La Lantejuela in Andalusia.

In his *History of Rome* Cassius Dio tells of a strange premonition that Gnaeus Pompeius had on the eve of the battle: "The eagles of Pompeius's legions shook their wings and let fall the thunderbolts which they held in their talons, in some cases of gold; thus they seemed to be hurling the threatened disaster directly at Pompeius and to be flying off of their own accord to Caesar. But he made light of it, for Destiny was leading him on; thus he established himself in the city of Munda in order to give battle."

As Caesar's legions rode into view and pitched their tents, Gnaeus Pompeius had his own 13 legions, as well as his cavalry, positioned on an open plain that led gradually uphill to the town. Both Titus Labienus and Attius Varus commanded troops on the field. Caesar, meanwhile, had eight legions and 8,000 cavalry. More than 120,000 men formed ranks on the battlefield that day.

Commentarii de Bello Hispaniensi (*Commentaries on the Spanish War*) provides some of the details of the lay of the land. The anonymous author notes,

> The two camps were divided from one another by a plain about five miles in extent, so that Pompeius, in consequence of the town's elevated position, and the nature of the country, enjoyed a double defense. Across this valley ran a rivulet,

which rendered the approach to the mountain extremely difficult, because it formed a deep morass on the right. Caesar had
no doubt that the enemy would descend into the plain and
come to a battle, when he saw them in array. This appeared
evident to all; [and it was significant] because the plain would
give their cavalry full room to act, and the day was so serene
and clear that the gods seemed to have sent it on purpose to
favor the engagement.

Excitement rippled through Caesar's legions as they drew up in
their battle formations. Legio V was on the left, and Legio X, with
Caesar himself, on the right, and the other legions comprising the
center. Caesar called the initial charge.

The massive battle befitted the ultimate contest of five years of
civil war. Both sides fought furiously, and Gnaeus Pompeius's men
made the most of their higher-ground advantage. Those on the
Optimate side who had once sworn allegiance to Caesar fought
the hardest in the exhausting and arduous conflict. They were well
aware of Caesar's having executed the opposing officers, whom
he perceived as treasonous, after his victory over Scipio less than
a year earlier at Thapsus. They, therefore, rationalized that dying
in battle would be preferable to the fate that awaited them if they
surrendered.

Cassius Dio notes that in the beginning, neither side gave ground.
He writes,

> Caesar and Pompeius, who witnessed these struggles from
> horseback from certain elevated positions, had no ground for
> either hope or despair, but, with their minds torn by doubts,
> were equally distressed by confidence and by fear. The battle
> was so evenly balanced that they suffered tortures at the sight
> as they strained to spy out some advantage, and shrank from
> discovering some setback. In mind, too, they suffered tortures,
> as they prayed for success and against misfortune, alternating
> between strength and fear.... Neither side for the moment
> turned to flight, but, matched in determination, they proved
> also to be matched in physical strength.

He adds that this drove both generals to dive into the fray. He reports:

> They were unable to endure it long, but leaped from their horses and joined in the conflict.... Thus they preferred to share in it by personal exertion and danger rather than by tension of spirit, and each hoped by his participation in the fight to turn the scale somehow in favor of his own troops; or, failing that, they wished to die with them. The leaders, then, took part in the battle themselves; yet no advantage came of this to either army. On the contrary, when the men saw their chiefs sharing their danger, a far greater disregard for their own death and eagerness for the destruction of their opponents seized both alike.

On the right wing, which Caesar himself commanded, Legio X finally collapsed the enemy's left. This forced Gnaeus Pompeius to pull troops from his own right to defend against a breakthrough by Legio X, but this so weakened his right that Caesar's left was able to punch through.

As the author of *Commentarii de Bello Hispaniensi* writes, "Upon this motion, [Caesar's] cavalry on the left fell upon Pompeius's right wing." When he saw Caesar's cavalry attack, Labienus led his cavalry to intercept them. However, when other troops saw Labienus doing this, they misinterpreted his move as a retreat. With that, cohesion within the Optimate lines collapsed, and an actual retreat did begin. As the anonymous author reports, "Though the enemy fought with the utmost vigor, they were obliged to give ground, and retire toward the town."

Those who took refuge inside Munda fought on bravely against the ensuing siege, but they were ultimately overwhelmed by Caesar's legions.

Plutarch writes that as Caesar was leaving the battlefield, he observed that this was the first time that he had to fight for his life in battle, telling "his friends that he had often striven for victory, but now first for his life."

Plutarch goes on to report that 30,000 of Pompeius's men were killed in action against only about 1,000 losses on Caesar's side.

Casualties may not have been that lopsided, but they probably were disproportionate and clearly were decisive. Both Labienus and Varus were found dead on the field, and the standards of all 13 enemy legions were taken.

As Plutarch summarizes the battle, Caesar "fought this victorious battle on the day of the festival of Bacchus, on which day also it is said that Pompey the Great had gone forth to the war....As for Pompey's sons, the younger made his escape, but after a few days the head of the elder [Gnaeus Pompeius] was brought in by Deidius."

Caesar then marched to besiege Corduba, which he was now able to capture. Sextus, who had been in Corduba on the day of the Battle of Munda, escaped, and was later seen leading Mediterranean pirates based in Sicily. He was caught by Octavian and executed in 35 BC, ten years after Munda.

Caesar returned to Rome in the early fall of 45 BC, where yet another Triumph was held in his honor, even though it was held to celebrate a victory over fellow Romans.

Plutarch notes,

> It vexed the Romans as nothing else had done. For it commemorated no victory over foreign commanders or barbarian kings, but the utter annihilation of the sons and the family of the mightiest of the Romans, who had fallen upon misfortune....However, the Romans gave way before the good fortune of the man and accepted the bit, and regarding the monarchy as a respite from the evils of the civil wars, they appointed him dictator perpetuo [dictator in perpetuity]. This was confessedly a tyranny, since the monarchy, besides the element of irresponsibility, now took on that of permanence.

The civil war was now over. It was the last of the many military campaigns waged by Julius Caesar.

Death and Legacy

As a general at Thapsus and Munda, Julius Caesar had been unforgiving to those who opposed him. When he returned home in the fall of 45 BC, Rome's dictator for life was the embodiment of generosity and magnanimity. He pardoned enemies and rewarded them as friends. Marcus Junius Brutus, for example, who had once been a staunch supporter of Pompey and the Optimates, had only to apologize to Caesar to be designated a praetor. In his will, which was not public knowledge until later, Caesar had even named Brutus as his heir, second only to young Octavian.

Even Pompey was treated charitably, albeit posthumously. As Plutarch writes in his biography of Caesar, "The statues of Pompey, which had been thrown down, he would not suffer to remain so, but set them up again, at which Cicero said that in setting up Pompey's statues Caesar firmly fixed his own."

Caesar certainly fixed his own mark on the future with a complete overhaul of the Roman calendar. He replaced the old Roman Republic calendar with his Julian calendar, which was aligned with the actual seasons and had a 365-day year, with a leap year every fourth year. Caesar's calendar was modified by Pope Gregory XIII in 1582 as the modern Gregorian calendar, but it is largely still with us today. The month of his birth is still called July in his honor.

The usually critical Plutarch was very much in awe of these efforts, writing,

> The adjustment of the calendar...and the correction of the irregularity in the computation of time, were not only studied scientifically by him, but also brought to completion, and proved to be of the highest utility. For not only in very ancient times was the relation of the lunar to the solar year in great confusion among the Romans, so that the sacrificial feasts and festivals, diverging gradually, at last fell in opposite seasons of the year,...but also at this time people generally had no way of computing the actual solar year.... Caesar laid the problem before the best philosophers and mathematicians, and out of the methods of correction which were already at hand compounded one of his own which was more accurate than any.

As popular as Caesar may have been with the people of Rome, dissatisfaction with him was growing in political circles. He behaved as a man above men, and even wore a ceremonial crown of laurel leaves wherever he went, although that may have been because of his baldness.

Cassius Dio reminds us in his *History of Rome* that the Senate "voted that [Caesar] should always ride, even in the city itself, wearing the triumphal dress, and should sit in his chair of state everywhere except at the games; for at those he received the privilege of watching the contests from the tribunes' benches in company with those who were tribunes at the time."

Cassius goes on to evenhandedly lay some blame on the senators, writing that Caesar "had aroused dislike that was not altogether unjustified, except insofar as it was the senators themselves who had by their novel and excessive honors encouraged him and puffed him up, only to find fault with him on this very account and to spread slanderous reports [of] how glad he was to accept them and how he behaved more haughtily as a result of them."

During the winter of 45–44 BC the political machinations against Caesar turned serious. Although the charismatic war hero retained the popular support of the majority of Romans, a conspiracy was afoot among political insiders to remove him.

The conspiracy to assassinate Caesar was led by Brutus and Gaius Cassius Longinus, a long-time political ally of Pompey's. Longinus's military experience consisted mainly of his being en route to Pontus to join Pharnaces II in 47 BC when Caesar tapped him to be part of his campaign against Pharnaces II. Around Brutus and Longinus were arrayed a cabal of about three dozen other like-minded senators, including Servilius Casca and Tillius Cimber, as well as Gaius Trebonius, who had been a loyal member of Caesar's officer corps throughout the campaigns in Gaul.

The day they picked was March 15, the Idus Martii (Ides of March), almost exactly one year after Caesar's victory at Munda. Plutarch writes that "a certain seer warned Caesar to be on his guard against a great peril on the day of the month of March which the Romans call the Ides; and when the day had come and Caesar was on his way to the senate-house, he greeted the seer with a jest and said: 'Well, the Ides of March are come,' and the seer said to him softly: 'Ay, they are come, but they are not gone.'"

Ironically, Caesar was on his way to an appearance at the Senate when he met the conspirators at the Theatrum Pompeium (Theater of Pompey), which had been dedicated to Caesar's rival in 52 BC. Suetonius writes,

> Cimber caught his toga by both shoulders; then as Caesar cried, 'Why, this is violence!' one of the Cascas stabbed him from one side just below the throat. Caesar caught Casca's arm and ran it through with his stylus, but as he tried to leap to his feet, he was stopped by another wound. When he saw that he was beset on every side by drawn daggers, he muffled his head in his robe, and at the same time drew down its lap to his feet with his left hand, in order to fall more decently, with the lower part of his body also covered. And in this way he was stabbed with three and twenty wounds.... Of so many wounds none turned out to be mortal, in the opinion of the physician Antistius, except the second one in the breast.

According to Suetonius, "Some have written that when Marcus Brutus rushed at him, he said in Greek, 'Kai su, teknon?' [You too, child?]." This was the reference to Caesar's having considered Brutus an heir that Shakespeare famously altered to "Et tu, Brute?" (And you, Brutus?).

In the wake of the assassination, Rome turned into chaos, and fires destroyed parts of the city. Caesar still had immense popularity with the masses, and there was an outpouring of anger against the perceived elitists who had done him in. Brutus and Cassius retreated to Greece with their supporters, much as Pompey had done five years earlier. Caesar's long-time second in command, Mark Antony, emerged as the most powerful man in Rome's political hierarchy.

However, to the surprise of most—especially Mark Antony, who thought of himself as Caesar's heir apparent—the assassinated dictator's will named the 18-year-old Octavian as his adopted son and the inheritor of his fortune. Demonstrating a political acumen unusual for his age, young Octavian moved to consolidate his power and was named to the Senate in January 43 BC at the age of just 19.

Also consolidating his power was Mark Antony, who demanded that the Senate give him control of Cisalpine Gaul, where Brutus had been named governor. Cicero moved to block this and succeeded in getting the Senate to denounce Antony as an enemy of the state the same month that Octavian became a member of the body.

In April 43 BC the two consuls, Aulus Hirtius and Gaius Vibius Pansa, assembled an army to march against Antony and gave Octavian *imperium,* or command, of the troops. When both consuls were killed in the fighting, the teenaged heir of Julius Caesar was sole commander of an army. In August he was named consul. In less than two years he had become a force to be reckoned with.

As consul he moved to have the conspirators in the assassination named enemies of the state. Also in that year he joined with Mark Antony and Marcus Aemilius Lepidus (shortly before his death Julius Caesar had named Lepidus his master of the horse) to form the Second Triumvirate. Unlike the First Triumvirate, this one was an officially formed entity that would last for a decade.

In case there was any doubt of the lasting popularity of Julius Caesar, early in 42 BC the Senate posthumously declared him a god, calling him Divus Iulius, or the deified Julius. Octavian therefore became known as Divi Filius, the son of a god.

A few months later, in October 42 BC, Octavian and Antony massed 28 legions in the long-awaited final showdown with Brutus and Cassius. This took place in two great battles at Philippi in Macedonia. When it was apparent that Octavian and Antony had prevailed, Cassius ordered an underling to kill him, and Brutus committed suicide.

Just as Julius Caesar had found himself in a civil war with another member of the First Triumvirate, Pompey, so too would Octavian find himself at odds with a member of the Second Triumvirate after it ended. He became embroiled in a conflict with Antony, who was by now married to the queen of the Nile, Cleopatra. The issue was Antony's plan to use the wealth of Egypt to finance his plan to take power in Rome and dominate its Mediterranean lands.

This civil war had its climax in the Battle of Actium in September 31 BC on a peninsula at the mouth of the Ambracian Gulf, only 200 miles south of Dyrrhachium, where Julius Caesar had his penultimate showdown with Pompey 17 years earlier.

When Antony lost at Actium, his fortunes declined, and his troops gradually began deserting. Because he thought that Cleopatra had been captured, and it had become clear that he would never defeat Octavian, Antony committed suicide. Less than two weeks later Cleopatra also killed herself. Octavian then ordered the assassination of Caesarion, the biological son of Julius Caesar and the political heir of his mother, Cleopatra.

Octavian, was granted a triple Triumph in 29 BC, and was elected to his third consulship, for a ten-year term, in January 27 BC. The Senate then bestowed the title Augustus, meaning majestic. In turn, he adopted the title imperator, meaning commander, and the root of the term *emperor*. With this the Roman Republic effectively became the Roman Empire, and Octavian, now called Gaius Julius Caesar Augustus, became the first Roman emperor.

The assassination of Julius Caesar had backfired. The conspirators had hoped to rid Rome of a perceived tyrant, but instead they brought about the end of the Roman Republic and accelerated the establishment of the Roman Empire.

Julius Caesar had essentially founded that empire and bequeathed it to his heir. But if the founder had lived, he had a bold agenda for future conquests.

Julius Caesar's military plans for 44 BC and beyond were quite grand. He had been planning to push the frontiers eastward, following the route of Alexander the Great into Parthia, the fringes of Persia; then he would have gone north into the Caucasus, and into Scythia, the steppes of Central Asia and Russia. He was well aware that the Scythians had stymied Alexander and he meant to outdo his role model.

After this Caesar's battle plan called for something Alexander never considered. He was going to turn back westward from Scythia, approaching Germania from the east, invading it as the Soviet army would in 1944 and 1945. With Rome already in control of Gaul, Caesar's legions would be like a hammer slamming the Germani against a Roman anvil on the west bank of the Rhine.

As Plutarch explains, "After overrunning the countries bordering on Germania and Germania itself, [he planned to] come back by way of Gaul to Italy, and so to complete this circuit of his empire, which would then be bounded on all sides by the ocean."

Closer to home, Plutarch writes, Caesar intended

> to divert the Tiber just below the city into a deep channel, give it a bend towards Circeium, and make it empty into the sea at Terracina, thus contriving for merchantmen a safe as well as an easy passage to Rome; and besides this, to convert marshes about Pomentinum and Setia into a plain which many thousands of men could cultivate; and further, to build moles which should barricade the sea where it was nearest to Rome, to clear away the hidden dangers on the shore of Ostia, and then construct harbors and roadsteads sufficient for the great fleets that would visit them. And all these things were in preparation.

This grand engineering vision remains unfulfilled.

Like all great conquerors, Julius Caesar thought big and acted big. Those who think big do not always achieve greatness, but those who think small never do. He was an exemplar of this.

He conquered all Gaul. He was the first Roman leader to lead a major force across the Rhine into Germania and across the English Channel into Britannia. In this he set the bar for future Roman conquerors. He challenged his successors to finish the job in Britannia, which they did to a substantial degree. He likewise challenged his successors to finish the job in Germania, which they failed to do.

He was arguably the greatest of the great Roman conquerors, and, though the title of emperor did not exist in his lifetime, it can be argued that Julius Caesar was the first and perhaps greatest among Rome's emperors.

As Suetonius summarizes, Julius Caesar "died in the fifty-sixth year of his age, and was numbered among the gods, not only by a formal decree, but also in the conviction of the common people. For at the first of the games which his heir Augustus gave in honor of his apotheosis, a comet shone for seven successive days, rising about the eleventh hour, and was believed to be the soul of Caesar, who had been taken to heaven; and this is why a star is set upon the crown of his head in his statue."

Today Julius Caesar is remembered as a man, albeit a great man, rather than as a god. Without his tenacious pursuit of the civil war, the Roman Republic would have eventually crumbled into fragments, and the Roman Empire would never have existed. Without Caesar's conquest of Gaul and expeditions into Britain and Germany, Roman civilization, including such defining influences of Western civilization as law, language, and engineering, would not have been ubiquitous in most of Europe.

Had there been no Julius Caesar, the world today would be unrecognizable.

Notes on Sources

IT HAS BEEN SAID THAT BOOKSHELVES GROAN UNDER THE WEIGHT OF various accounts of the lives of history's greatest people. With Julius Caesar it would be no exaggeration to say that entire libraries groan under the weight of nonfiction works in which he is featured— which is not to mention works of fiction, especially the hundreds of editions of William Shakespeare's immortal sixteenth-century play in which Julius Caesar is the title character.

All historical works about Caesar are based in whole or in part on the writings of five ancient authors, one of whom is Julius Caesar himself. Unlike many of the great figures of antiquity, Caesar wrote his own accounts of his two most important campaigns in *Commentarii de Bello Gallico* (*Commentaries on the Gallic War*) and *Commentarii de Bello Civili* (*Commentaries on the Civil War*). Three other sets of commentaries have been attributed to him, though they are now thought to be the works of someone else. These cover aspects of the civil war campaigns and include *Commentarii de Bello Alexandrino* (*Commentaries on the Alexandria War*), *Commentarii de Bello Africo* (*Commentaries on the African War*), and *Commentarii de Bello Hispaniensi* (*Commentaries on the War in Spain*).

The other four historians who wrote more or less contemporary accounts of Caesar's exploits are Appianus, Cassius Dio, Plutarch, and Suetonius. The first two wrote of Caesar in the context of their histories of Rome and its empire. The last two wrote specific biographies of Caesar, each part of a larger series of biographies of Roman leaders.

Appianus of Alexandria, also known as Appian, was an ethnically Greek citizen of Rome who lived from about AD 95 to roughly AD 165. His coverage of Caesar is in books 13 through 17 of his *Historia Romana* (*Roman History,* or *History of Rome*). They are considered to be among the best original sources on the history of the Roman Civil War.

Lucius Cassius Dio Cocceianus, known as Cassius Dio, was the son of Senator Cassius Apronianus. His mother was a relative, perhaps daughter, of the Greek orator and philosopher Dio Chrysostom. Cassius Dio wrote his own extensive *Historia Romana,* an 80-volume work covering 1,400 years of Roman history; the earlier volumes survive only as fragments. Cassius Dio was born at about the time of Appianus's death; served as a senator, governor of Smyrna, and later as a consul; and died in about AD 229.

Lucius Mestrius Plutarchus (circa AD 46–120), better known as Plutarch, was one of the most prolific writers of his age. This Greek historian was a naturalized Roman citizen, best known for his *Lives of Noble Greeks and Romans,* aka *Parallel Lives,* a collection of biographies of more than four dozen notable individuals, including Alexander the Great and Julius Caesar.

Gaius Suetonius Tranquillus was born in the eighth decade of the first century, the son of Suetonius Laetus, who hailed from Hippo Regius (now in Algeria). Gaius Suetonius Tranquillus is thought to have died some time after AD 130. He was also a close friend of the senator and historian Gaius Plinius Caecilius Secundus, known as Pliny the Younger. Suetonius is best known for writing the 12-volume *De Vita Caesarum* (*On the Life of the Caesars*), usually called *The Twelve Caesars.* Published in AD 121, it is a series of comprehensive biographies of Julius Caesar and the first 11 Roman emperors—Augustus, Tiberius, Caligula, Claudius, Nero, Galba, Otho, Vitellius, Vespasian, Titus, and Domitian. The first volume, the biography of Julius Caesar, is *Vita Divi Iuli* (*The Life of the Deified Julius*) and was written in about AD 110.

A fifth historian whom I cite in this book is Gaius Plinius Secundus, better known as Pliny the Elder, whose *Naturalis Historia*

(*Natural History*) was a massive encyclopedia published around AD 77. In it he attempted to encompass all the world's knowledge.

For the history of the Germans in this period, against whom Caesar campaigned vigorously, the best primary source is *De Origine et Situ Germanorum* (*The Origin and Situation of the Germans*), also called *Germania,* by Publius Cornelius Tacitus and originally published in Rome in about 98 AD.

In writing this book I used various editions and translations of the works of the five original sources. For Appianus, Cassius Dio, and Suetonius, I used the English translations by Horace White, Earnest Cary, and J. C. Rolfe, respectively, all published as part of the Loeb Classical Library, beginning in 1913, and now under the auspices of the Harvard University Press. For Plutarch, I used the multi-volume edition of *Parallel Lives* translated by Bernadotte Perrin for the Loeb Classical Library. The volume containing Plutarch's biography of Caesar's principal rival, Gnaeus Pompeius Magnus (Pompey the Great), was published in 1917. The volume containing his biography of Caesar was published in 1919.

For works by Caesar himself I consulted the edition of *Commentaries on the Gallic War* translated by W. A. McDevitte and W. S. Bohn published by Harper in New York in 1869. For the *Commentaries on the Civil War* I used both the McDevitte-Bohn edition, also published by Harper in 1869, as well as the translation by William Duncan published in St. Louis by Edwards and Bushnell in 1856.

For *Germania* by Publius Cornelius Tacitus, I used the translation by Alfred John Church and William Jackson Brodribb first published in London by Macmillan in 1876.

Index